THE PERFECT MATCH: Pairing Delicious Recipes with Great Wine

by Brian St. Pierre

the author of *A Perfect Glass of Wine*

PHOTOGRAPHS BY E. J. ARMSTRONG

CHRONICLE BOOKS
SAN FRANCISCO

Text copyright © 2001 by Brian St. Pierre. Photographs copyright © 2001 by E. J. Armstrong. All rights reserved.

No part of this book may be reproduced in any form without written permission from the publisher.

Library of Congress Cataloging-in-Publication Data available. ISBN 0-8118-2918-9

Printed in Hong Kong.

Design and typesetting by Em Dash, San Francisco.

Food Styling by Patty Whittmann. Photo Design by Andrea Austin.

Distributed in Canada by Raincoast Books, 9050 Shaughnessy Street, Vancouver, BC V6P 6E5

1 3 5 7 9 10 8 6 4 2

Chronicle Books LLC, 85 Second Street, San Francisco, California 94105

www.chroniclebooks.com

To my wife, Sarah, who has the recipe

ACKNOWLEDGMENTS For recipes, advice, tips, and techniques, my thanks to Piero Antinori and the staff at Cantinetta Antinori, Florence, Italy; Jean-Luc Colombo, wine maker and great cook, Tain l'Hermitage, France; Rita Compagnoni, in Sestre Levante, Liguria, Italy; Jamie Davies, Schramsberg Vineyards, Napa Valley, California; Shaun Hill, Merchant House, Ludlow, England; Matt Kramer, who lives in Portland, Oregon, but left his heart in the mountains of Italy's Piedmont region; Maureen Lolonis, of Lolonis Winery in Mendocino, California; Teresa Severini Lungarotti, of Cantine Lungarotti, Torgiano, Perugia, Italy, where the family also runs Le Tre Vaselle, a distinguished restaurant; Mary Etta Moose, my old friend and collaborator, now at Moose's in San Francisco's North Beach; Nick Pierano, chef-owner of Nick's Italian Cafe, in McMinnville, Oregon; Château Ste. Michelle Winery, Woodinville, Washington, for a recipe from *John Sarich at Chateau Ste. Michelle: For Cooks Who Love Wine,* by John Sarich, © 1997, published by Sasquatch Books. Also, thanks to Giles Kime, who as an editor of the *Sunday Telegraph* in London commissioned articles containing several of these recipes, and *Decanter* magazine in London, which has provided me with resources and a forum in which to work out a lot of perfect matches over the years.

~BRIAN ST. PIERRE

Photography on a project this size is never the work of just the photographer. In this book I had a number of people who went beyond normal professional expectations. First and foremost, my food stylist Patty Whittmann and photo designer Andrea Austin, who worked constantly to make the work a cohesive vision. A special thanks to Dan McCarthy of McCarthy and Schiering Wine Merchants for his gentle advice and props from his personal collection. Thanks to Bitters of Fremont, Seattle, for giving us free rein of the place. Thanks to Pottery Barn for loaning us lots of props even in the busy holiday season. As always, throughout my photos are the props from Antique Liquidators which Carl, Janice, and Matt continue to supply me with. Others who contributed and are not to be missed are my assistants Birgit Walbaum and Rachael Arnold, who make things just that much easier.

~E. JANE ARMSTRONG

INTRODUCTION: WHY WINE?

Grapes are amazingly complex little packages, containing everything necessary to turn themselves into wine, proving to a lot of people that this is why they exist. Certainly, grapes are good to eat fresh or dried, but it's really all the flavors and goodness of their fermented juice—their best use by far, surely—that has spread them around the world for more than six thousand years, with vines growing in every country in the temperate zones, on mountainsides and desert flats, as far north as Canada and down to the southern tip of Africa, thriving across continents and cultures. Wine has flowed through history, helping define gastronomy, surviving snobbery and fads, and becoming the stuff of legend—quite a load to bear for something that most often simply asks for nothing more than a quiet place at the dinner table.

"A meal without wine is like a day without sunshine," wrote Jean Anthelme Brillat-Savarin, and he was right. Wine completes a meal like nothing else can. Water has its place, of course—with ice cream, or to keep you alive in the desert, but that's about it. Soda and coffee have the wrong flavors for almost any sort of food except possibly hot dogs and pastries; tea runs out of possibilities outside Chinese restaurants; beer just suffices to wash away the heat of chilies and curries and the saltiness of chips or nuts. None of them has the range of flavors to fit so many foods as wine; none is much of an aid to digestion, the way wine is (its acid balance is close to that of your stomach); and none of them is anywhere near as tasty, let alone as interesting.

This book is about making the most of those flavors, getting the maximum enjoyment from food and wine. There are some who say it doesn't bear thinking about, that matching food and wine is only a matter of using good-enough wine, and letting the rest take care of itself, which is like saying that seasoning doesn't matter, just use salt or pepper, garlic or onions, whatever you feel like. Others, at the opposite end of the scale, propose wine and food matches with pinpoint precision: "With duck à l'orange, only a Château Blather from the very best year of the last decade will do." They never advise you what to do if you can't find any Château Blather, though: Starve? Have a sandwich for dinner?

The simple and very pleasant truth is that there are usually several wines that go quite well with almost any dish; what's important is that they are within close range of each other, and that some sort of delicious synergy is set up with food. Wine exists to enhance food, and all good wine does that. There's at least one wine for almost every food, and in most cases there are several. The quest is to find them, which gets easier with the understanding of some basics.

When a grape is converted into wine, several things happen. The skins release *tannin* into the juice; tannin is a preservative, present in the skins of all fruit. The softer the fruit, the more need for tannin, which is why peach skins can taste dried out and neutral and apple skins don't. With grapes, the tannin helps to keep the juice (and the wine) from spoiling. The trade-off is that the wine will be astringent and mouth-puckering for a while: a few months for most whites, and a few years for many reds, whose skins have more tannin.

The sugar in the grape is converted into alcohol when the juice ferments. Alcohol is also a preservative, and it also affects the flavor of the wine (it also affects your judgment, coordination, and libido, I know, but I'm presuming moderate consumption). If the sugar content of the grapes is high and the juice is fermented to a sugar level of nearly zero, that is to say complete dryness, the wine will be quite alcoholic and have a somewhat hot, harsh aftertaste. Some wines from warm-weather areas, like much of California, Australia, southern France, and Italy, can be as much as 14 percent alcohol or more these days, which translates to big, overblown, often heavy sensations that clobber your palate—they don't sing to you, they yell, and they can certainly drown out what food's got to say, so it's important to note the alcohol content on the label.

The other important component of wine is acid, which should create a balance with the sugar in the grape to begin with (wine makers often decide when the grapes are truly ripe by simply tasting them), and retain a balance with the fruit flavor of the particular grape variety all the way through the wine making. All fruits have acid, which is another preservative, but is also critical for flavor: A Granny Smith apple is more interesting and pleasant than a Golden Delicious, for example, because it has more firmness and acidity; its flavor and texture are crisp and refreshing. Acidity is very important in wine. It's less obvious in reds, because they have more complex and heavier flavors than whites, but it's vital. A wine that's low in acid will be flabby, with no zip, nothing to stimulate and refresh your palate, and to set you up for the next sip or bite.

Put them all together, and you have something simple enough to be enjoyed, complicated enough to be judged. You can go further, and think about things like texture and weight (smooth or rough, light or heavy in your mouth); what people in the wine trade call length (persistence of the flavor); varietal character (what grape it's made from); and bouquet, breeding, polish, and other nuances. Or, you can stop with a basic understanding and an open appreciation of that delicious synergy between food and wine, which will provide enough of the real pleasures of the table. Either way, you can't lose.

WHAT'S THE BIG IDEA?

Spanish ayes: an infinite variety
Italy: celebrating diversity
France: elegant, inspired evolutions

FOOD AND WINE: WHAT'S THE BIG IDEA?

Even as recently as twenty years ago, there were restaurants out in the countryside in Italy and Spain where, when you sat down and ordered a meal, you would simply be asked if you wanted wine with it, and if you answered yes, a carafe and glasses would be brought. The carafe would be decorated with the abrasions of a thousand washings, and the glasses would not be stemware; the wine would probably be red, and certainly local. If you had asked for a wine list, your eye would have been directed to a few bottles lined up on a shelf behind the bar, probably slightly dusty. If, having taken a few bites and a sip, you had commented on how well the food and wine complemented each other, you would have drawn the same sort of brief, indifferent look you'd have gotten if you had announced that the earth was undoubtedly round.

Today, there's likely to be a dubbed version of *Friends* showing on the TV above the bar, stemmed glasses, and a printed wine list, and the owner's son or daughter may be happy to chat with you about California wine, having learned some English in preparation for a trip to the Napa Valley last summer. What will be unchanged will be the perfect matches among the local food and wines, still taken for granted, as well they should be: They've grown up together in the same neighborhood for hundreds of years, part of the same culture, evolving within the same traditions. As we'll see, they have a lot to tell us, too.

Grapevines don't look like much, however and wherever they're cultivated, but they're actually remarkably sophisticated plants. They're tough and adaptable, with a complex genetic system that makes them among the best survivors in the world, weaving their way through our history for at least six thousand years, carried along by beasts and birds and then quite far by man, from some central point near the Mediterranean to as far west, eventually, as England and as far east as China, and across all the world's oceans. Like so many immigrants, the grapes did whatever was necessary to suit their new homes, seducing us with intriguing new flavors and adapting by mutating repeatedly: the Pinot family, for instance, includes Noir (red), Blanc (white), Gris (pinkish), Meunier (red, but made as white in the cooler Champagne district), and possibly Tempranillo, the great red grape of Rioja in Spain. Vines also lent themselves to natural selection by farmers: Some female vines need male vines to reproduce, but there are hermaphroditic vines that can go it alone (and thus save vineyard space), so they're the ones you see in "wine country" today.

When wine was made long ago, it often had to be tinkered with—stabilized, preserved, flavored—and so our palates had to adapt, too. Sometimes, it was a practical matter, as when the Greeks discovered that some pine resin added to a jar of wine kept it from spoiling, and so gave the world the marginal pleasure of retsina, which was at least better than vinegar; sometimes it was fashion, as when a sweet-toothed king decreed that wine should be honeyed or spiced, and the royal court nodded assent and joined in. As wine making slowly became more scientific, the tinkering got more subtle, and imposed less on the grapes' flavor. The interplay of vineyard and wine became more a matter of terrain and climate and culture, which link up endlessly with the food chain. Whichever is the chicken and which the egg, there will always be a beverage, and it will suit.

Take retsina for a moment, as a good example of flavor synergy. It's still made by including gobs of pine resin with the crushed grapes as they begin to ferment, and when it's done, it is pungently piney. You have to be either passionately Greek or powerfully thirsty to drink it by itself. However, have a sip with a wedge of spanakopita, the spinach–feta cheese–onion pie, and you get the point of why retsina has lasted for a couple of thousand years: with

tannin (spinach), salty tang (feta), and sulfurous bite (onion), you need something that is equally tangy and bites back. Portuguese *vinho verde* is another example; it's "green" in the sense of being made from slightly unripe grapes, and quite tart, even sour. It's another killer to drink, pucker-power personified. But try it with a platter of somewhat oily and strongly flavored grilled sardines, or a hotly spicy stew of tripe, beans, and sausages, and you will find that it's a match.

These are extremes of flavor. Most of the time, we edge closer to the middle ground, where most main dishes are found. In America, we approach the whole matter of gastronomy and the food supply from a different direction from Europeans: We arrive pretty much from above—we're can-do, we're democratic, we can suit ourselves, and so we do. We control, adapt, modify, mix, and match from the greatest selection of food and wine anyone anywhere has ever known. Our gastronomic choices are amazingly broad, maybe too much so, considering that we have little history and hardly any training, compared with Europe, which has been fine-tuning delicious solutions for centuries. If we're going to get the most out of our bonanza of choice, Europe is a good place to look for guidance.

NATURAL SELECTIONS

Spain, Italy, and France, the countries where wine is the most integral to the cuisine, also happen to be the ones with the most interesting and complex array of food. They also have quite individualistic ways of consuming it.

Spain is famous for *paella*, the spicy dish of rice, meat, and shellfish, and for dinner at 10 or 11 P.M., a custom that makes American tourists feel as if they've got permanent jet lag. (I can recall a week in Madrid where I had dinner every night at 9 o'clock, almost alone in a restaurant, except for a few self-conscious American or Japanese tourists; I'd finish around 10:30, just as the Spaniards were beginning to settle in.) In fact, Spain's gastronomy is as richly layered as its history. It's a cuisine of ingenuity, of endless, sophisticated variations on combinations of humble ingredients.

The rhythms of Spain and the rest of southern Europe are different from the steady, prudent Anglo-Saxon cadences most of us have grown up with, the steady progression of our slow march through a good, solid breakfast high in fiber and fruit; a coffee break; a light, one-course lunch with a sensible beverage; perhaps a drink and a snack after work; dinner; and to bed after the ten o'clock news. In southern Europe, the day starts with a series of quick small cups of strong coffee and chat at standup coffee bars, with an occasional pastry to keep you going until early afternoon, when the snacks become savory bits of meat, fish, cheese, or eggs and bread and short glasses of wine, then a multicourse lunch, followed by a siesta, a bit more work, and then the grand walkabout—the *paseo* in Spain and the *passeggiata* in Italy—when the whole town turns out for a stroll (which makes for quite a throng perambulating in Madrid!).

They stop and chat on the street, sit at a sidewalk café and have a glass of something and a nibble of some tapas from small plates, chat some more, move on, sip and nibble and chat again, for a couple of hours. They enjoy each other, and they've brought the concept of hanging out to a fine art. Anywhere else, so many people drinking in the street might be cause for alarm; here, it's just socializing. Then, finally, it's time for dinner, a procession of dishes served in a leisurely way.

In terms of climate, "southern" Spain is really most of the country, warmed by hot winds from Africa across the narrowest part of the Mediterranean, and by the sun on the large plateau of the middle interior. Life (and food) is structured around climate: hard work in the mornings before the sun takes over the day, fueled by coffee and light pastries that won't slow you down; more substantial snacks of preserved meats and fish and cheese with a small glass of wine as the morning ends; a rewarding full-fledged lunch and a nap at the peak of the heat; a measured series of snacks and a few glasses of sherry to stimulate the appetite during the stroll and the gossip; and then, when the day is at last cool, dinner.

Paella is wonderful, but only a small part of Spanish gastronomy. Tapas, the inventive procession of savory snacks, is more revealing. The Spanish always eat when they drink, and the range of food, served in small dishes, is extraordinary: blanched or fried almonds; several kinds of olives; strips of salt cod in batter; grilled sardines and other small fish; fried prawns; ham and other kinds of cured pork; grilled or fried vegetables stuffed with or wrapped around each other or both; a variety of spicy sausages; chunks of octopus; hot or cold squid; marinated mushrooms; cheese plain or cooked; potatoes in garlicky tomato sauce; fritters of all sorts; meatballs; and tortillas, which in Spain are potato and onion omelets, rather like dense quiches, cut into cubes, served cold, and a nice counterpoint to all the spicy stuff. (The word *tapa* means "lid," from the small saucers or thin slices of bread that were originally placed over the top of the glass to keep out dust and bugs, and obviously handy for holding a few nuts or olives or slices of sausage to nibble between sips. Waiters sometimes keep track of your bill by stacking the saucers at one side of your table.)

Only one wine could keep good company with the range of tapas on offer, and that is sherry, especially the light, bone-dry type known as *fino*. It's strong, more than 15 percent alcohol, and deliberately oxidized, so it has a very mature, distinctively tangy, yeasty, slightly nutty flavor; it's served chilled, in small glasses, about 3 ounces a serving. It tastes good, certainly, but its flavor, being slightly pungent and uncomplicated, could seem monotonous after a while on its own; spicy or pungent food, however, refreshes it (and vice versa).

In most wine-producing areas of the world, the local wine is supreme, naturally, but in most of Spain, no matter what table wine is available, the evening belongs to sherry, because of tapas. Both began in the hot southern area of Andalusia (another well-known dish of the area is gazpacho, the cold soup of tomatoes, peppers, and cucumbers, and one of the few soups that goes well with wine—sherry, of course). You even encounter this sherry culture in Logrono, the capital city of Rioja, fiercely proud home of Spain's most famous red wine, on the Calle de los Laureles. The street is lined with tapas bars and small restaurants—there seem to be no other businesses for several blocks—and the air is an exotic muddle of smells, rich and enticing. One place is known for the best fish tapas, that one's for sausages, another specializes

in ham and pork, and across the street there are hot tapas, little dishes of stewed meats and meatballs in spicy sauce. You discover that sherry suits them all as you wander along, one contented soldier in a large, ravenous army indulging in what really is a movable feast. Later, you'll have a red Rioja with spit-roasted lamb or duck, or a full-bodied, acidic white Rioja with *zarzuela*, a stew made from fish added to the pot one at a time in a sequence of timing that keeps all their flavors and textures individual, and they will be wonderful, but what you'll remember longest will be the sherry and the tapas and the *paseo*, the heart of the matter, a perfect marriage of wine and food and conviviality.

LAND OF WINE

Italy was a collection of city/states and independent republics for most of its long history, becoming unified as a nation only in 1861. It has had more than fifty governments since it became a republic in 1946, and produces more than a thousand types of wine. Obviously, the idea of "unity" is relative.

Still, this is the country that gave the world some of the first cookbooks, invented ice cream, gave pasta and coffee to the rest of Europe, and forks, broccoli, artichokes, peas, good table manners, and *haute cuisine* to the French. The ancient Greeks called Italy "Enotria," the land of wine. When Venice ruled the Mediterranean and controlled the spice trade with North Africa, Genoa was sending seagoing merchants to the Atlantic ports of Europe, and Tuscan princes were sending a wine known as "Florence red" to England in exchange for wool; that was in the fifteenth century, quite a head start on the rest of the world.

Italians will tell you, quite happily, that there is no such thing as "Italian food," just a long culinary misunderstanding begun in America by the first waves of immigrant restaurateurs from the south, with their tomato sauces and pizzas. It's regions that matter, they say. An emphasis in the last two decades on "northern" cooking, with the introduction of risotto, polenta, simpler presentations of pasta, and an array of fish dishes, has corrected the balance a bit, and more regional differences are emerging here, reflecting the reality there.

In most of Italy, meals are a procession of dishes, each element quite separate, not thrown together on one plate, as we eat, and certainly not rushed. In restaurants, it's assumed that you will begin with an antipasto (one or more appetizers—the word means "before the pasta"). Then, of course, you'll have pasta, then a choice of fish or meats, and vegetables (*contorni*). You can order the vegetables when you order the meat, and you may get them at the same time, as a side plate, or they may appear before or after the main course. There will then be cheese, and possibly after that, fruit, and, finally, dessert; the dessert list will usually include sweet wines. (Americans who sit down and order a salad and fish send waiters and chefs into tailspins of despondency.) Even in a private home, where there may only be three courses and some fruit afterwards, it unfolds easily in a sequence, each part to be enjoyed at leisure.

Look at the long coastline, and you will assume, correctly, that fish is important in many regions, but the best fish are sold to city markets, and much of the cooking along the shores of the eastern provinces, from the heel of the Italian boot almost to Venice, is hearty soups and stews made from several kinds of humble fish: hake, rockfish, sardines, anchovies, scorpion fish, gurnard and other bottom feeders, along with cuttlefish, octopus, and squid. Monkfish used to thrive before they became popular, but are now overfished and rare. The Sicilians, out in the middle of the Mediterranean, have more choices, bringing in swordfish and tuna, and creating memorably flavorful dishes (sun-baked Sicily has always been known for its vivid flavors, and its heady, strong wines were often sent north to blend vigor into the wines.

The wines of Italy have changed radically since the 1960s, when much of their history was swept aside. New regulations went into effect then, and have been vigorously overhauled several times since. In southern and central Italy, white wines were often based on Trebbiano and Malvasia, grapes that can grow in poor soil and produce a large crop but produce wines that are mediocre, not distinctively flavored, high in alcohol, fairly acidic—and probably suitable for some of those rustic fish stews, but not much else. One solution was to make them slightly sweet, so they would be more generally palatable. It's not much of a tradition, to be sure, and one based more on poverty than any other imperative, so not very instructive for us. Those wines, such as Verdicchio (which used to be sold in fish-shaped bottles) and Frascati, were at least agreeable; thirty years ago, they were the whites you saw in Italian-American restaurants, along with amiable but forgettable Orvieto. The reds, also high in acidity but usually light and reasonably fresh, and with some more distinctive flavors, were more likely to be valued on Italian shores.

Modern wine-making technology has changed the situation. Cool fermentation in stainless-steel tanks coaxes a little fruitiness out of the grapes and controls the acidity, so there are more wines that are better than merely agreeable now, and dry. Trebbiano is being phased out in some places in favor of Chardonnay. In Sicily and Apulia—the heel of the boot—the native varieties are often blended with Merlot or Chardonnay, producing palatable but only moderately interesting wines aimed at the export market. The offbeat native varieties are being coaxed along for a more discerning local market.

Red grapes are tougher in every way; many different varieties thrive well enough to be accepted where they are, not so subject to replacement in modern times as whites: Wines like Rosso Conero, Aglianico del Vulture, and especially Primitivo, which turns out to be the ancestor of California's Zinfandel, are well suited to the ingenious vegetable combinations and straight-forwardly spiced pastas of the south.

Things are better, and more instructive, farther north, where prosperity brought refinement of ingredients, cookery, and wine. In northeastern Italy, the hills and mountains above Venice provide white Pinot Grigio, Soave, and Pinot Bianco, as well as red Valpolicella, Amarone, and good Bardolino. Here there is also a concentration of French varieties, like Cabernet Sauvignon, Merlot, and Chardonnay, which have been established for more than a hundred years—some goes to cosmopolitan restaurants

in Milan, a symbol (for most Italians) of international snootiness, or for export to America. The sparkling wine from here, Prosecco, is quite appealing.

Venice has long memories of economic and gastronomic supremacy, of reveling in sheer style and flair. Both freshwater and saltwater fish are available here; the Venetians claim more versions of risotto than anyone else; they adore sweet-and-sour sauces and spice mixes from their trading days with the Arabs; and they elevated polenta above peasant food. The fish here includes scampi, sole, crab, and elegantly prepared salt cod, which they match with excellent Pinot Grigio, or often good Soave or Pinot Bianco. Tender calf's liver or quail are perfect with light, fresh Valpolicella or Bardolino. On the slopes of the Alps north and west of Venice, the cooking is somewhat influenced by Austria and Yugoslavia, which fought over the territory for centuries, and by the cooler climate: Pumpkins and mushrooms abound, the range of vegetables make this Italy's most sophisticated garden, meats are braised in milk or wine, gnocchi are the favored starch, and the same wines apply, beautifully. People are spoiled here; the Orient Express runs through the valley, quite an appropriate symbol.

Tuscany seems to be everybody's idea of Italy these days, home of expatriate authors and Italy's most famous wine, Chianti. Other Italians call Tuscans *mangiafagioli*, "bean-eaters," a jibe at the simplicity of their cuisine, and quite unfair. A snack or appetizer here is *crostini*, toasted bread rubbed with garlic and olive oil, and smeared with vegetable purees or chicken livers. The steak here is from the huge white cows of the Chianina breed, served as tender two-pound slabs, always grilled and invariably blood rare. The chicken is split, flattened, marinated in olive oil and wine, rubbed with herbs, and grilled; the pasta is served with sauce of rabbit or duck meat; the soups are vegetable and as dense as stew. These are all dishes made for Chianti or its more muscular cousin from southern Tuscany, Brunello di Montalcino. To the east, in Pisa and Lucca and its coastal towns, more seafood enters the equation, along with the persistently refreshing white, Vernaccia di San Gimignano.

Up in the northwest corner of the country, Piedmont is the gastronomic peak of Italy, though not so well known everywhere as such because its principal city, Turin, doesn't offer a lot of

reasons to visit, and the rest of the area is mountainous and full of small towns. It's the home of Italy's best wine, Barolo, and its second-best wine, Barbaresco, as well as one of the best known wines in the world, Asti Spumante, and one of the most misunderstood, vermouth. The fabulous white truffles grow only here, deeply flavored fontina cheese originates here, and the wild mushrooms from the deep valleys are among the best anywhere. Piedmont shares the Alps with France and was once part of that country; the cuisine is a rare combination of aristocratic tradition and robust country cooking that takes advantage of an abundance of superb ingredients.

The Piedmontese will ask you, as a kind of test, what kind of wine you'd prefer. Answer simply "red," and you have passed. They make Dolcetto and Barbera, both named for the grape—with extensions for the area where they're produced (Barbera d'Alba, and so on)—for everyday meals or casual occasions, or some-times to begin a grand meal, with the appetizers. There are several different whites made from ancient native varieties, well above the average Italian standard, but they don't seem to be taken terribly seriously. Many end up in restaurants on the Ligurian coast, where seafood reigns. Asti Spumante is a popular export.

Piedmont is also, unsurprisingly, the headquarters of the Slow Food movement ("for the Defense of and Right to Pleasure"), which has more than ten thousand members and chapters in fifteen countries, including the United States. The organization publishes books and magazines on food and wine, organizes gastronomically extravagant conferences, encourages artisanal food producers and farmers' markets, and may yet save us all.

LAND OF HOPE AND GLORY

France is way out in front when it comes to a culture of hand-in-glove food and wine. Some people these days accuse French chefs and wine makers of coasting on past glories, but even if they were, that's still a long line of accomplishment. The French have taught a lot of the rest of the world how to cook and eat, and their well-defined ideas are still the foundations even of the "new cuisines" of other countries. They've also transported their grapes, which have become the basis of the wine industries of California, Washington, Oregon, Australia, New Zealand, South

Africa, Chile, and Argentina, all of which they still call "the New World." Gastronomically, their influence on the American melting pot has been considerable.

Their lofty position doesn't seem to be because their aristocracy was more gifted, or even simply more aristocratic and elegant than others; in the Middle Ages, their feudal systems and agriculture weren't necessarily superior, and they shuttled their fair share of princes and princesses back and forth in the political marriage exchanges of Europe, which helped spread the niceties of culture. A century later, they were slow to accept American food such as peppers, tomatoes, potatoes, and corn, and they never have done much with rice, either. On the other hand, their conservatism meant they went deeper with what they did value, and they hung on to their various cuisines long enough to evolve and fine-tune them to an extraordinary degree.

They also cherished the differences among their cuisines. French cookery is even more sharply defined within the different regions than Italian, and the wines are quite divergent, each a strong part of the region's identity. They even have a word for it, of course: *terroir*. Literally, it means "soil," or "homeland," but gastronomically, it stands for the ecological basis of agriculture, the combination of the character of the soil, rainfall, sunshine, wind, and temperatures that gives that corner of the planet, and therefore its apples or artichokes or cheese or wine, its specialness. It is a word spoken reverently, and it has passed into the language of wine making everywhere, so that an Italian vintner is as likely to tell you about his *terroir* as a wine maker from the Napa Valley. (There is certainly something to it, as you can see in tasting Pinot Noirs, say, from New Zealand, Oregon, and California alongside red Burgundy; they're obviously siblings, but not the same, and Burgundy is still considered to be the model.)

Another reason for the elevated position of French cuisine is simply that they demand it. Every country gets the cuisine it deserves, after all, and a tradition of culinary supremacy, even if it's partly based on myth, drives all before it. The French are probably the world's greatest complainers: An aggrieved Frenchman, especially in a restaurant, intransigent and apoplectic, is an awesome sight. On the other hand, consider the British:

FRANCE

champagne
alsace
chateau de chambord
bergundy
atlantic ocean   mont blanc
sarlat
bordeaux
mediterranean sea

FOOD AND WINE

They form a line without being asked, they are polite, and they hate making a fuss. Their food? For much of their history, it's been the most abysmal stuff imaginable, a worldwide joke.

The French cuisine that even the French think of as their comfort food is that of Burgundy. A light dances in their eyes and they smile broadly when they talk of that food, so abundantly and honestly flavored. Even someone from Bordeaux, who may not know much about the wines of Burgundy, will quickly become warmly sentimental about the food: the chickens of Burgundy (*poulets Bresse,* with their own official appellation of origin), or the cheese, sausages, cherries, and especially the wonderful gingerbread. Some perennial old favorites like snails in garlic butter; the mustard Dijon gave the world; *coq au vin;* and *jambon persillé,* the rich terrine of ham and parsley, have become so familiar everywhere that their origins in Burgundy are often forgotten. It's substantial food, and cooking that's thoroughly sophisticated, but not fussy.

Much Burgundian cooking is based on wine, even the egg dishes: Here you'll find *ouefs en meurette,* eggs poached with bacon in red-wine sauce, quite delicious, though lacking in eye appeal. They make beef *bourguignon* and beef *à la bourguignonne,* the former being browned cubes of meat in red wine and the latter a whole piece of meat in red wine and brandy; they simmer a stew of various river fish in white wine; and even the meat in the sausages is steeped in wine before being stuffed into casings. Nothing goes to waste, ingeniously: Chicken is cooked in the sour juice of unripe grapes in early summer, when the vines are pruned for a better crop, and at harvest time in the autumn, fruit may be poached in the thick dregs of pulp and juice left after the grapes are crushed.

The wines encourage the food. Many people consider red and white Burgundies to be the best wines in the world in good vintages. The reds are made from the Pinot Noir grapes and the whites from Chardonnay, and they're the models wine makers all over the world aspire to emulate. The climate of Burgundy is somewhat cool, and the wines have a lively streak of acidity running through them, as well as subtle, unforced power: They're wines made for food that is naturally richly flavored.

Sumptuous eating and drinking continues uninterrupted as you go south, through Lyon and down through the valley of the Rhône River, one of France's great waterways, cleaving through the landscape all the way through Provence to Marseilles and the Mediterranean Sea. On the mountainous slopes, terraces hold the vines that yield sturdy Hermitage and Châteauneuf-du-Pape wines. Here, olive oil replaces butter in the kitchen, and the ratatouille, the garlicky mayonnaise, the salt cod brandade, and the bouillabaisse all demand lusty, voluptuous red wines or, at least, on a hot day, one of their vibrant, tangy rosés, which are some of the few pink wines worth bothering about.

Up in the northeast corner of the country, Alsace has the most sharply defined cooking and wines in France. It lies behind a mountain range that gives it an easy climate, alongside the Rhine River across from Germany, and it has been a battleground and possession of both countries for hundreds of years. The language here is full of Teutonic words or echoes of them, and the food overlaps the two countries, except that many feel the Alsatians do it best: noodles; dumplings; several kinds of cabbage, especially sauerkraut; roast goose (they stuff it with sausage and drench it with wine); pâtés, terrines, and every other type of *charcuterie;* quiches and sweet tarts and other pastries. It's gastronomic heaven.

This is serious white-wine country, and the wines not only take the name of the grapes, but the most notable ones are different from those of the rest of France: Riesling and Pinot Gris and Gewürztraminer. Fairly high in alcohol and acidity, they are lean and stronger than their counterparts in Germany or Italy. Alsatians eat a lot of game and meat, strongly flavored, but the wine is a supple partner in a dance that has evolved into an intricate pattern. Their chicken-and-wine dish, *coq au Riesling,* is simmered in a wine-and-cream sauce and served on buttered noodles; *choucroute garnie* is a mix of sausages and pork soaked in sauerkraut and Riesling, served with boiled potatoes; the snails are simmered in Riesling; their pungent Münster cheese is used in everything from soup to sauce, and eaten dipped in cumin seeds; the specialty stew, *baeckeofe,* is made from unbrowned beef and pork marinated in Riesling, which they also drink with it. What all these foods have in common is direct, persistent flavor and, especially, a smooth texture, which isn't a bad way of describing the wine, either.

Bordeaux is on the gastronomic map more because of its wine than anything else. It's the land of merchant princes, and sometimes just merchants who could afford to build grand châteaux and ships to carry their wines around the world. The food is relatively simple: The Atlantic coast and several deep rivers provide oysters, mussels, eels, crayfish, and other light fish to go with the white wines blended from Sauvignon Blanc and Semillon, while lamb, steak, duck, geese, kidneys, and rabbit are grilled or roasted, and just about hold their own with the usually strong and astringent local wines, blended from Cabernet Sauvignon, Merlot, and a few other grapes. They make far more red than white wine, which may account for the fact that they also have quite a few fish stews using red, which actually taste pretty good once you get used to the unusual flavor. The term *à la bordelaise* ("Bordeaux style") has always been rather vague, and now usually signifies simply that the food in question has been cooked in red wine.

At the châteaux, cuisine is a different story, rather grand: Dinner may start with an intensely sweet Sauternes paired with foie gras, move on to a delicate crayfish mousse and a smooth ten-year-old white wine, then to rare slices of roast lamb covered in sauce of wild mushrooms and truffles with a twenty-year-old red wine. The same menu has been served for most of the last century in grand restaurants in New York, London, and Paris, its success measured to a great extent by the age and glory of the wine, which plays the same role as the soloist in a concerto: the only instrumentalist in the orchestra who is as important as the conductor. There seem always to have been two Bordeaux, gastronomically, and no middle ground. Either way, though, there's always been enough of the right wine.

BACK HOME

There are many more examples in Europe, all the way down to specific neighborhoods and cooks. Over the centuries, both wine and food have evolved according to a variety of dictates, whether it was availability or fashion or politics or prosperity, but they invariably evolve together, with consistency and harmony. It may be a harmony that strikes us as odd, like starting a meal with Sauternes and salty pâté or Roquefort cheese, but we can't say it doesn't work in context, that is, in Bordeaux (and it does taste good, if too rich to do very often). On the other hand, that high-acid wine that tasted so good and so right on the beach in Portugal with those grilled fish and that spicy stew may just be a vicious shriek across your palate back home, especially with elegant salmon and a subtle roast chicken with thyme and mashed potatoes. People often say that a certain wine "doesn't travel well," but actually it isn't the wine, it's the culture.

America has never really had a wine-oriented culture, or the sort of ingrained food and wine traditions southern Europe enjoys, but that's not a problem—instead, it's an extraordinary opportunity. We can write anything we'd like on this blank slate.

There's another important point to consider, with great pleasure: America has quite a few pretty good regional cuisines, too. There may not be an evolved wine tradition to go with them in all cases, but making perfect matches is easier than ever, given all the options. Whether we're re-creating New Orleans or New England cooking, Midwest or Southwest, there are not only hundreds of Merlots and Chardonnays or Zinfandels and Sauvignon Blancs, there are also red and white Burgundies, Pinot Grigios, Soaves, Barberas, dry and slightly sweet Rieslings—a whole array of choices for every cuisine.

In this most eclectic, free-ranging marketplace, all you need to decide is just what you want from wine, and it will be there. This book is a road map of flavors, with classic recipes and contemporary variations that have been selected to provide the foundations for integrating food and wine pleasurably and to give directions for further explorations, however far you want to go. There are no barriers or boundaries, and it's bound to be a long, lovely trip.

MATCHING UP: A MATTER OF TASTE

I have a book I really treasure, bought for a few cents off a used-book table somewhere, titled *London at Table: or How, When and Where to Dine and Order a Dinner, and Where to Avoid Dining*. It was published in 1851, at the peak of the Industrial Revolution, when England was "the workshop of the world," economically supreme and reveling in it. The word *Victorian* had begun to be used as an expression of proud self-consciousness, and a generation of newly wealthy businessmen and their wives discovered dining as status symbol and entertainment, at home as well as in grand restaurants. Able at last to afford servants and conspicuous consumption, they changed the fashion from serve-yourself buffets to stately, seated dinners, multicourse processions accompanied with an array of wines.

They almost had it all, lacking only the confidence of those who have grown up with easeful luxuries. A new industry was created for them, of social arbiters and writers of etiquette books who could help social climbers up the aspirational ladder. These gastronomic enforcers dealt with the *nouveaux riches* sternly, by staring them down and never blinking. Rules were the lash with which they whipped the newcomers into shape, administered with a kind of vinegary satisfaction.

"In order to give the cook fair play, the fish should *never* be served with the soup—it is a distinct and important course," snaps the anonymous author of *London at Table*, going on to warn of various "vulgarisms" to be avoided, before getting around to the etiquette of wine in a way that leaves no wiggle room: With soup, "hand round Madeira and Sherry; and remember that, after turtle, punch is banned from all well-regulated tables." With white fish, "one glass only of Hock or Moselle cup [a kind of punch, combining Riesling and Sherry]. With salmon, either Claret cup [another punch], Claret, or Port." Here, there is a footnote explaining that the "rule" about white wine and white sauces with white fish, and red wine and brown sauces with brown fish, also applies to white and red meats. Champagne may be served throughout to the females at table, as it's "a favorite with the ladies, a prevailing weakness of the day," but even so, *not* with the roast. Claret cup or port is served with game (we are still within one meal here). Cherry brandy is served after dessert. Oysters may be served at the beginning or end of the meal, accompanied with either Chablis or Sauternes. Cheese is out, apparently because it would have to be served from one platter, and be handed round, thus not elegant.

Aside from the weird mix of flavors and the endurance test of alcoholic strengths, what is striking here is the extraordinary assurance of this rather arbitrary dogma. Perhaps that was what carried this sort of self-help industry forward into the next century, and across the ocean to America, where the same awkward mix of prosperity and insecurity was rising.

As eating got simpler in modern times, quite a few of the more outrageous "rules" fell away naturally, but I can certainly recall, even into the 1960s and 1970s, being told in no uncertain terms that you served red wine with meat, white with fish, and rosé with ham or as a compromise if you couldn't agree on red or white (one big wine company in California even put pictures of meat on the labels of their red wines, and fish on the whites). The rules may have been simplified, but they were still rigorously asserted.

ROLES, RULES, AND MYTHS

Even when it was still crude stuff, wine had a mystique about it, attracting fads and fashionable ideas and myths. The Greeks and Romans knew about some of its medical and nutritional benefits, and discovered that it could sometimes get better with age. Ancient Egyptians had a classification system for vintages and vineyards, and buried their kings with jars of wine for the journey to the next life. Sometimes, it was flavored with honey, spices, pine tar, and onions or leeks (thought to have medicinal value); often, it was made full-bodied and high in alcohol, then cut with water to precise measures according to the occasion or the season, or perhaps the custom. Whatever the variations, there was one constant: Wine was the beverage for meals and celebrations.

There aren't any useful comparisons to be made between the food and wine of today and those of times far past, but there are a couple of persistent myths. One was that using wine in cooking could lead to alcoholism if done regularly, a misconception that still pops up from time to time. The fact is that alcohol is highly volatile and evaporates very quickly; those who worry about kids getting a taste for wine at an early age should know that the taste of wine in cooking changes too, blending with and adapting other flavors. There is also a long-standing myth about marinating meat, poultry, and fish in wine. It's often said that this tenderizes them. Not so. There isn't any substance in wine that could do that. Wine can add moisture to the surface of the meat, but if you were to marinate a tough steak for a long time in Merlot, you'd just end up with a tough purple steak. (Wine does add some flavor, though, and helps the flavor of herbs and spices to permeate food, so it's a useful marinade from that angle.)

The worst myth is the somewhat dumbing-down notion that any modern wine goes with any food. Of course, it's an over-reaction against all those rigid rules, but I suspect that it's also perpetrated by people who can't cook. Saying that you can drink any wine with any food is just like saying you can cook any food without salt, pepper, or other seasonings: It's technically true, but why would you want to do it?

Let me tell you a story. Once when I was doing a charity promotion in Vancouver, I was invited to dinner by one of the benefactors. The restaurant was the best in town, with great food and a fabulous wine list, and my host was a multimillionaire known as a serious gourmet, so I was quite looking forward to it. When I arrived, he announced that he only drank one wine, since once he'd found the wine he liked he saw no need to ever try any others, but that I needn't worry, it was one of the world's best wines. He was right. The wine was Dom Perignon, and we drank that great Champagne right through the meal, which featured voluptuously sauced game birds and rich, rare beef. It cost a lot of money, and the food was wonderful, and it was an ordeal: The wine wilted through all those mismatches, and the food seemed clumsy, like a large man dancing with a small girl.

There is no substitute for tasting with an open mind, on any level of experience. At *Decanter*, the wine magazine I write for most often, we have a food-and-wine tasting every month at a restaurant, with writers, restaurateurs, chefs, and wine merchants eating and drinking their way through various cuisines and propositions: What wine with Chinese food, what food with Riesling, what wine with cheese, that sort of thing—basically, good fun for wine professionals, with a moderately serious spirit of inquiry among the good-natured arguments. One tasting, lately, was on white wine and red meat. We tried a dozen wines, from full-bodied Chardonnay to Pinot Grigio and delicate Riesling, with six beef and lamb dishes and seven sauces. A pretty-hot Thai beef salad went well with German Riesling, and a couple of other combinations weren't bad, but we all had to agree that, in the end, our minds kept drifting to various red wines as better matches, and certainly a lot more fun to drink with the food.

So it seems, after participating in several of these sessions and experimenting a lot on my own, that the conventional wisdom isn't bad advice after all, as long as it's taken just as informal advice, as the starting point for getting the most pleasure out of wine instead of being the final verdict in a closed system. Pinot Noir with salmon or a classic *coq au vin* is a perfectly good idea, and there are those who would say that Chardonnay is also a winner with those dishes, but there are also quite a few who'd

say that either with either, depending on your mood or preference, is the best idea of all. There are always more wines under the umbrella of pleasurable companionship than outside it.

WHAT'S IN A NAME?

This is as good a place as any to try and clear up some points of wine labeling. Most wine from California, Australia, New Zealand, Chile, and South Africa (which Europeans still insist on lumping together as "the New World") are labeled with the name of the grape it was made from or, if the wine is a blend, at least the principal grape in that blend. The idea is that you will then have a pretty good idea of the basic flavor of the wine in the bottle. Of course, there will be variations, due to the soil and climate where the grapes were grown, and often there will be differences of style imposed by creative wine makers, but if the wine is honestly made, there will be a good family resemblance among, say, Chardonnays from Australia, Chile, and California.

In Europe, which has much more variable climates among the different regions, wines have generally tended to be named for the place where they come from, on the theory that the amount of sunshine or the quality of the soil was what mattered most; the grapes weren't named, because they were usually all the same—Chardonnay in Chablis, or Pinot Noir in Burgundy, for example, or Riesling in much of Germany—or combined in similar blends, as in Chianti or Bordeaux or Rioja. Within each category, there will be a strong family resemblance, and there will also be some resemblance among the Europeans and their cousins from the New World: Red Burgundy and Oregon or California Pinot Noir, for example, will have some of the same flavors, but also some interesting differences. The best way to discover your preferences among this delicious diversity is also the most pleasant, by tasting them.

MODERN STYLE: WHAT'S NEW?

Even as recently as twenty years ago, a fair amount of wine was made under somewhat primitive conditions, using methods that hadn't changed in hundreds of years. These days, even in developing nations, wine is usually made in highly sanitary conditions, in antiseptic stainless-steel tanks, with carefully temperature-controlled crushing of the grapes and fermentation of their juice, all monitored by computers twenty-four hours a day, seven days a week. Modern wine is clean, sound, reliable stuff most of the time, which makes evaluating and using it a simpler matter than ever. Here are some highlights of what to look out for:

Alcohol is one aspect that matters a lot. There's generally more of it in modern wine. In the old days, wine was fermented in big open tanks, and when its sugar was converted to alcohol, some of it evaporated; these days, in those nice clean stainless-steel tanks, which happen to be closed, there's no natural blowing-off. Also, and I'm serious, there's global warming. Heat means more sugar in the grapes as they ripen, and that translates to higher levels of alcohol after they ferment (in Napa and Sonoma, for example, average sugar levels at harvest time have increased enough in the last two decades to add almost 2 percent of alcohol to many of their wines).

Whatever the reasons, a higher alcohol content not only means the wine packs more of a punch, but it affects the flavor. A wine with a delicate fruit character, like Riesling or Pinot Noir, can seem hot and rough at 13 percent alcohol (most Rieslings from Germany, where it's still pretty cool, weigh in at 10 or 11 percent; about 12 percent is a good, restrained average for wines from elsewhere). Chardonnay at 13.5 or 14 percent alcohol is going to be fairly muscle-bound, certainly not subtle at all. Wines with more ample fruit flavors, like Zinfandel and Cabernet Sauvignon, can balance the alcohol more easily at 13 or 14 percent, but at that level, they are certainly big, bold wines, so you may want to think twice about serving them with food with subtle or elegantly complex flavors.

Oak is another slightly controversial aspect of flavor in modern wine. Wine used to be made in large casks or vats, and the inexpensive stuff either went straight to bottling or was aged a little while in medium-sized casks; the expensive ones went into small oak barrels for a longer time, where they acquired a bit of oaky flavor, adding some complexity. Mainly, the extra character they got was roundness and mellowness from maturity in the barrels, but the slight taste of that oak became a hallmark of first-rate, expensive wine. So, someone ingenious came up with the idea of adding small pieces of oak to wine that was made in stainless steel, to provide that flavor without the time-consuming maturation process; unfortunately, some of the mellowness sometimes got lost in the process. Wine that is excessively oaked, either from oak chips or from being stored for long periods in new oak barrels, can taste woody, dried out, and astringent, and may overpower subtle food. The flaw is most often found in Chardonnay, so it's a good idea to taste it before serving with fish, shellfish, or poultry.

Tannin is important as a preservative for most fruit and some vegetables—you've encountered it as the slightly papery taste of the skin of peaches or pears, and the astringency of tea. It's in grape skins and seeds, too, and when the grapes are crushed, it passes into the wine, one of the reasons why so many red wines age so well. It can come across as a harsh taste in young wines, especially notable in Cabernet Sauvignon—the wine can seem hard, ungenerous, and puckery—but it fades with age. A two-year-old Cabernet may be like a punch in the mouth (and it's impossible to think of any suitable food to go with it), but a ten-year-old version can be glorious, mellow, rounded, and complex, with a lasting flavor, a fine companion to red meat and game.

Acidity might sound daunting, but it's really a prime attribute, quite natural and essential in many kinds of fruit. It's one of the factors that contribute to wine's balance: Too much and a wine can seem sour, too little and it's flat and lifeless, but the right amount makes it lively, crisp, and refreshing. All wines have it, but acidity is especially valuable in white wines, which are low in tannin and other compounds that make red wines complex and interesting. Good fruit character and vibrant acidity are often enough to make a white wine intriguing, and a splendid companion for a wide variety of food.

⌒ WHEN PLANNING A MEAL WITH WINE, IT'S IMPORTANT TO LOOK AT THE
WHOLE PLATE, NOT JUST THE MEAT AND SAUCE, BUT THE VEGETABLES, TOO.

WHAT'S COOKING?

Cooking any liquid reduces its volume, and intensifies its flavor, which is why we're always advised to use unsalted stock for risottos and stews, for example. It's the same with wine: Any flaws or imbalances will be intensified in the final dish, so it's important to taste a wine before pouring it into the pot.

One "rule" in those early dogmatic advice books that used to drive me crazy was the one that said, "Always cook with the same wine you will be drinking." I think the first time it struck me as impossibly dumb was when I was making a beef stew that required two cups of wine, which was going to be served with a very expensive Burgundy—nearly half a bottle of this precious stuff going into the pot? No way!

I've tested this idea at home, and we re-created it in a *Decanter* magazine workshop. Half a dozen versions of the same recipe were cooked, using the same ingredients but each using a different wine, from downright cheap to quite expensive. Most downright cheap wines tend to be either slightly sweet or somewhat bland, and those are the characteristics that showed up in the final dish. On the other hand, expensive wines tend to be markedly flavored (red wines will be tannic and slightly harsh, and whites may be oaky and strongly acidic, all characteristics that will fade with age but make them difficult when they're young). The best wines, in general, tended to be those just a step or two up from the cheapest: "California" appellation jug wines and Vin du Pays d'Oc from the south of France were the most reliable. So, the inescapable conclusion was, save your best stuff for your glass, not the pan.

There's another point worth making: The longer the dish was cooked, the more the wine's character faded. So, for stew, the wine is less important than it is for a quick sauté or deglazed sauce. Beyond that, the other consideration can be the type of wine you'll be drinking: An elegant white Burgundy or Carneros Chardonnay in your glass and a California or Vin du Pays

Chardonnay in the pan is an easy way to approach the question, and for a more informal sort of dinner with a more casual wine, simply opt for a dry wine that tastes good.

One wine that's often overlooked is dry vermouth. It's much maligned because of all the jokes made by Martini drinkers, who treat it as if it were a necessary evil, but it has a place in the kitchen. Vermouth is dry white wine, of average quality, which has been steeped with herbs and various spices and seasonings. As a drink, it can be an interesting mixer, but more importantly, it's pretty good in the pot, intriguing and offbeat, lending a lightly spicy hint to wine sauces. It's an old chef's secret—try some and see.

The other question that arises about cooking with wine concerns color. It's not all that relevant. White wine is better than no wine in a beef stew, though red is better. White wine in meat or mushroom risotto doesn't cancel out red to drink with it—often white wine is used in various sauces and stocks because red would discolor the food.

When planning a meal with wine, it's important to look at the whole plate, not just the meat and sauce, but the vegetables, too. A lightly sautéed fillet of white fish, such as petrale or sand dabs, that you want to serve with a light white wine like an Italian Pinot Grigio, may be rudely jostled by spinach (which tends to be tannic) or Brussels sprouts (which can be sulfurous). Creamy mashed potatoes, with a little aromatic thyme stirred in, and a fennel or butternut squash gratin, will sing in four-part harmony. On the other hand, that spinach will fit in well with garlicky roasted potatoes, a leg of lamb, and some hefty Zinfandel or Barolo. Balance, always, is the key.

In a restaurant, it's not always possible to reconcile wine with exotic or offbeat food. If you're the host, seek help from the waiter, and try to make the best possible compromise, accepting the fact that it is going to be a compromise; if the food's that exotic, it's not going to be a great wine occasion anyway, and if it's exotic and really good, there's no point in letting wine complicate the pleasure. Simplicity is often the best solution.

COLD COMFORT

What about cold meats: leftovers or light lunches from the deli, including sandwiches? The best wine to serve with cold roast beef, chicken or turkey, ham or roast pork, and even cold sausages, is a fairly dry German Riesling. The combination of fruit and acidity in a good German Riesling is perfect with the subtle flavors of cold meat: the scale of meat and wine is just right. Alsace Riesling, being drier and higher in acidity and alcohol, works less well; Chardonnay and other big wines are hopeless, overbearingly out of whack.

Spicy salami, in whatever style, works better with light red wines that have good fruit and just a touch of acidity. Beaujolais and Merlot go well with a range of Italian salamis, especially the unaged versions, while slightly more tart wines like Dolcetto and Chinon go better with the aged, harder types and the garlicky versions from France as well as Italy.

BREATHING ROOM

Another bit of conventional wisdom that just won't go away is that wine must be allowed to "breathe." Waiters in fancy restaurants will ask, "Shall I open the red wine now and let it breathe?" Or they offer, in a perfunctory tone that makes it clear that this is imperative, to pour the wine into a decanter, so it can "breathe" even better. I've also had meals with people who, knowing my profession, apologize for serving the wine out of the bottle, as they don't have a decanter. If I can drive a stake through the heart of this muddled cliché once and for all, I'll be very happy. Plainly put, the cliché is wrong.

Wine does benefit from contact with air, but not in the ways it has been supposed. A professional panel for *Decanter* magazine tested the proposition thoroughly, a tedious process of tasting wines that had been decanted for five hours, two hours, and a few minutes before serving, as well as just opening the wines and letting them stand for five hours, two hours, and a few minutes before serving. The wines were tasted "blind," that is,

without seeing the labels, so any affection or prejudice about the actual wines would not come into it. There were several types of white wines in one test, and then a quartet of red Bordeaux in another, and when the scores were tallied up, everyone was surprised.

For white wines, the only clear result was that oaky Chardonnay lost some of its woody taste after it was decanted for a couple of hours. Otherwise, there were few perceptible or consistent results with any of the other varieties, regardless of when they were opened or whether they were decanted.

For red wines, the flavor comparisons were quite poor when the wines were aired longest, either decanted or just opened five hours ahead, which we are often advised to do by some experts; in fact, in most cases, "allowing the wines to breathe" didn't really do them much good. *The best result, in general, came when the wines were simply opened and poured.*

That's not to say that some exposure to air doesn't help. The place where wine blossoms and opens up is in your glass. Use a good-sized glass, at least 8 ounces, and only pour it half full, and within a few minutes the wine will release its aromas and begin to soften a bit, ready to provide as much pleasure as it can.

WHAT'S THE PROBLEM?

It must be admitted: Some foods don't go well with wine; some just quibble over the finer points of getting along, while some argue and misbehave quite badly. There aren't that many of them, however, and the incompatibility isn't always that severe: This corner of the whole wine business is so small that it isn't really as much of a problem as many people have been led to believe. The conflicts usually arise from an overbearing aspect of the food (only occasionally is it the wine), and the solutions are simple, usually a matter of moderation, modification, or in a few cases, avoidance. There is rarely any great loss of pleasure involved. Here's a rundown of the usual suspects, reasons for a lack of harmony, and some commonsense advice:

Artichokes contain a compound that can make wine taste quite sweet, or sometimes metallic. It's most pronounced in fresh artichokes, but barely noticeable in artichokes packed in oil, Italian style, so if you want them in a dish served with wine, that's the way to include them. Otherwise, I've always found the messy business of eating a fresh artichoke complicated enough not to involve a glass of anything anyway.

Asparagus contains an amino acid that is very similar to a compound in wine that results from spoilage—not a very nice association. Fresh asparagus is glorious, not to be missed, so do as the Italians do, and serve it as a separate course, without wine.

The cabbage family, which includes broccoli, Brussels sprouts, cauliflower, and turnips, is high in sulfur; when cooked, they release various sulfurous compounds that not only don't smell good, but also pass the unfortunate effects on to wine. For cabbage, either skip it or go for low-sulfur varieties like napa cabbage or red cabbage, cook them lightly, and mix with wine-friendly matchmakers like carrots or caramelized onions; for cauliflower, try sprinkling them with sugar and slow-cooking them with unsalted butter; for turnips, serve them raw in salad, julienned. For broccoli and Brussels sprouts, skip them.

Chocolate is a good example of perception and reality in the food-and-wine game. Those who love chocolate tend to find more good matches than those who don't; it used to be said that chocolate was a no-no, but then the Belgians and Italians and Swiss moved us all into their dark, bittersweet realms, and forever changed the equation. People who really like chocolate (by which I mean the dark kind, not milk chocolate) say that it goes well with port, Cabernet Sauvignon, and even Asti Spumante. I have never seen such people moved off that position, so I think that deciding whether there's a conflict depends on deciding how you feel about chocolate first. Everything else will surely follow from that point onward.

Eggs are often cited, but common sense about occasions (such as breakfast) should tell us it's quite a minor problem. Eggs also contain sulfur, but not as much as they did in the days before cold storage, when this bugaboo was propounded (and back then, wine contained a lot more sulfur than it does now). Texture's probably a worse problem in some cases—I can't imagine getting pleasure out of eating a soft-boiled or fried egg with wine. On the other hand, a good, fluffy omelet and a glass of wine is a terrific lunch.

Vinegar is, of course, a problem, as its sharp acidity overwhelms wine. It's most pronounced in its natural state, as in salad dressings, so you can either serve the salad as a separate course without wine, or substitute lemon juice for the vinegar in the dressing, or mix half as much vinegar with the same amount of wine (in both those cases, it's also a good idea to use lighter or flavored oil, such as a blend of olive oil and walnut oil). Thai salad dressing, with its otherwise wonderful mix of sweet-sour-hot-salty flavor, is even more hopeless with wine. In cooked food, such as tomatoes, prolonged cooking and the addition of caramelized onions or a couple of good pinches of sugar can mitigate the acidity.

Otherwise, most conflicts come up because of strong flavors, such as the heat of chilies in Mexican, Thai, or Indian food, and of mustard and horseradish with meats, the vinegar in sweet-sour dishes and relishes such as chutneys, and the saltiness of teriyaki. The usual advice used to be to drink beer, but beer doesn't have really compatible flavors; it's mainly cold and wet, so it doesn't add to your pleasure. Low tannins can minimize clashes with hot spiciness and salt, so easygoing whites and casual reds often work, which brings up another important point: A lot of conflicts occur on a fairly minor plane, where the food doesn't ruin the wine, just pushes it around, adds or takes away an edge. Often, serving simpler wines—which have fewer nuances to be blunted—is the answer.

As I said at the start, this really is a minor set of concerns. Everyone's palate and perceptions are different. Moderation is important in creating balances. Above all, refer back to your own palate. Taste. Try things when you're on your own, and see what works for you—the good surprises are really worth it, and life's too short not to get as many of those as you can.

RISING TO THE OCCASION

One important aspect of wine that's not often mentioned is where and when it's being served: What, in other words, is the occasion? Picnic, backyard barbecue, weekend lunch, a supper of leftovers, a dinner party? Each has its own level of commitment, formality, and expense, but how do you judge where wine comes in? My general rule is, serve the best wine that you can afford. My wife, who is far more practical, has modified it brilliantly, as she points out that there are three categories of people you'll entertain: the ones you like (friends, lovers, perhaps family), the ones you are obliged to have in (neighbors, business associates, paybacks, perhaps family), and the ones you don't care for but have to (your boss, someone you owe, perhaps family). Thus, Sarah's very sound rule is, serve the best wine that you can afford *that fits the occasion and the category.*

The other occasion that matters is when you're alone, in which case the best idea is to follow the example of my friend Sam Deitsch, who always cooks himself a first-rate meal from scratch and has a nice wine with it, on the principle that you should always do the best you can for the person you love most.

The other question that comes up about entertaining is, how much is enough? A 750-milliliter bottle holds just over 26 ounces, and the usual serving for table wine is 4 or 5 ounces per glass (3 ounces for sweet dessert wines). So calculate on that basis: For a dinner party, a glass of wine when guests arrive, one with appetizers or a first course, two with the main course, and a small one with dessert, which amounts to a total of about two-thirds of a bottle each. Over the space of two hours and with food to slow the absorption of the alcohol, that's not too much for someone who isn't driving. (It's always a good idea to have some food available, whatever the occasion. It's also always a good idea to have wine in reserve, in case some is spilled or spoiled.)

For receptions or a buffet, you can serve fairly ordinary wine, as long as it tastes good; people are more prepared to tolerate ordinary wine when standing up than when sitting down, when they're able to concentrate more on it. The only exception is Champagne; there's no excuse for serving mediocre Champagne.

DOING DINNER

My wife and I do a lot of entertaining, in the form of informal dinner parties. Done right, they're wonderfully convivial; done wrong, they're sheer hell. Here are some guidelines for creating a successful occasion:

~ Make sure you have enough glasses.
  Never double them up—who needs to stop everything while you wash and dry them to pour another wine? Rent extras if you have to.

~ Write down a timetable for the food preparation.
  Don't assume you'll have everything done. Write it all down, be realistic about the timing, and then add 10 minutes to every step for insurance. Make sure the final step ends at least 20 minutes before guests are supposed to arrive, so you have time to relax.

~ Allow enough time for the white wines to be chilled properly.

~ Have all the reds standing upright, in case they have any sediment, which will sink to the bottom of the bottle.

~ Set the table in advance.

~ Wear comfortable shoes while you cook.
  I'm not kidding—nothing tires you out like hurting feet.

~ You can never have enough ice.
  You can't rely on the fridge, and never put wine in the freezer—it's not an efficient way to cool wine, and one day you'll forget it's in there. A bottle of white wine will chill well in half an hour in ice, more than twice that in the fridge; several bottles of wine will take even longer. Allow at least 1 hour in ice for any more than 4 bottles.

~ Make as much as possible ahead.
  This is where a cold first course comes in handy, and if dessert is made ahead too, then you only have to worry about the conversation and the main course. If there is any advance preparation possible for the main course, like chopping vegetables or making a sauce base, or even just premeasuring herbs and spices, do it.

THE BIG CHEESE QUESTION

Wine and cheese are natural allies, being the product of similar fermentations, but there are enough significant differences to make the affinity more like a cordially wary relationship than a real marriage.

I was brought up taking cheese seriously; for example, it was never questioned that strong red wine would be matched with cheese at the end of a formal meal, whatever the cuisine in question: Port and Stilton, Amarone and Gorgonzola, very old Rioja with Manchego, Bordeaux with aged Cheddar or Colby, that sort of thing. The idea, basically, was that after working your way up through white wine with the fish and red wine with the meat, you had to keep going on in that direction. As it turns out after a lot of tasting and thinking about it, I've had to conclude that the idea of matching red wine with cheese, basically, doesn't really work much of the time.

A big part of the equation is tannin (in the wine) and acidity (in both). Red wine, being high in tannin unless it's quite well aged, can taste bitter with a lot of pungent or salty cheeses, or simply lose its edge and taste a bit flat with some soft cheeses. Dry white wines tend to do a little better, as their acidity can make a good fit with higher-acid cheeses like goat cheese, or work as a contrast with good, creamy Brie or Münster.

The combination that works best, indisputably, is sweet wine with strong, salty cheese. The classic choice is Sauternes and Roquefort, although the other two great blue cheeses, Gorgonzola and Stilton, also match it quite well. The key here is the sweetness, as well as richness: This is a big bang of an ending to a meal. Even though it's red and higher in alcohol, port, also rich and sweet, is just as good with all three; the key is the sweetness level and

the underlying acidity (in Normandy, where they don't make wine but grow great apples, they often serve cider with cheese, and it works well enough if the cider's fairly sweet). Super-sweet late-harvest German Rieslings, those on the Trockenbeerenauslese level, also work well. A little of either will go a long way. The appeal of the cheese with the wine is that the wine by itself can tire your palate—too much of a good thing. The contrast of the cheese keeps it interesting.

Below that level of richness, the matter of choice becomes rather more subjective. A slightly sweet white wine offers the most possibilities, something like a German Riesling on the Auslese level, Coteaux du Layon from the Loire Valley, Recioto di Soave from Italy, late-harvest Rieslings from California or Alsace, and late-harvest Gewürztraminer from Alsace. A few fortified whites are also light enough to fit well here, including the lightly spicy Muscat de Beaumes de Venise and some Sicilian Muscats. A smooth tawny port is also a contender.

The advantage of serving lighter and moderately sweet white wines like these with cheese is that it gives a meal something of an upturn in terms of flavor and ends the meal on a lighter note than when a big red is served. (It also makes it easier to move on to dessert, if you are going to.) Limit the cheeses served to three—say, a goat cheese, a blue, and a Gruyère. If you really have to serve a red, do as they do in Bordeaux and serve a mature Gouda, which is a nice middle-of-the-road firm cheese.

A WORLD OF WINE FLAVORS

Here are the principal varieties and categories of wine produced in most of the world, organized largely by color and weight and intensity of flavor. Some, like Chardonnay and Merlot, have escaped national boundaries and adapted themselves nicely all over the world, although sometimes still retaining enough of an accent to stand out from the international-style chorus. Some others, like the Australian blends, go their own odd way, resembling nothing else, which makes a certain amount of aesthetic and cultural sense, even if it wasn't planned that way. The main thing is, though, that however any of these wines got where they did, there is a good range of partners for most of them.

Matching wine and food isn't really a difficult or complicated task. It's really a matter of logic and taste, and rules or rigidity shouldn't come into it. If the food is spicy or tart, for example, a wine that is spicy or tart stands a good chance of creating sensory overload; if the food is robustly flavored, like lamb shanks simmered in red wine with mushrooms, a delicate wine is going to be flattened by it. The important thing is that the wine enhances the food: Grilled meat or chicken, or even fish, is going to be caramelized and perhaps a little smoky, and demands a wine with a smooth, refreshing character; bland food, such as poached fish or baked chicken, will be perked up by a crisp, lively wine. In this section, I've outlined the character and principal flavors of the most popular varieties of wine from around the world, and related them to various compatible kinds of food. In the next section, I use recipes to make the same points from a different angle, and in more detail.

CHAMPAGNE

Champagne is often the first wine we encounter on many occasions, as a welcoming glass or a pre-dinner drink, so it's a good place to start. Most of our associations with it are of celebration and luxury rather than food (except for an almost automatic linkup with caviar), but there are plenty of good, lighthearted possibilities.

Good Champagne is made mostly from noble grape varieties, like Chardonnay and Pinot Noir, and has considerable character and nuance. The types seen most often are Brut, which is the usual dry blend of those two grapes and sometimes a little Pinot Meunier or Pinot Blanc; Blanc de Blancs, made from Chardonnay and also quite dry; or Blanc de Noirs, white wine with a slight copper tinge, made from Pinot Noir and Meunier and also quite dry. Pink Champagne, which can be made from red grapes, as is rosé, or which may have had a little red wine added to white, tends to have a bit more body, but has the same dryness level. Real Champagne comes from France and is strictly regulated; California Champagne doesn't and isn't, but the versions made from Chardonnay and Pinot Noir in the cool regions of Anderson Valley in Mendocino, Carneros in Napa and Sonoma, Russian River in Sonoma, and up in some of the hills between Napa and Sonoma often deserve the same measure of respect. Read the back labels, which provide a lot of clues; ask a good wine merchant for recommendations of these classic-variety wines made by the classic Champagne method; and be prepared to pay a premium (cheap "Champagnes" are never a bargain).

Aside from the bubbles, the hallmark of Champagne is its crisp, tart acidity, which provides a bracing cut of considerable refreshment, and enough intriguing nuances to keep you coming back for more: Good Champagne is never one-dimensional. The best wines come from the coolest areas, where the grapes barely ripen, so they retain that nice bite of early-season fruit; the nuances come from skillful blending of wines from several vintages, which builds up subtle layers of complexity.

People have built whole dinners around Champagne, which is sort of fun in an "it's-good-to-be-the-king" way once in a while, but Champagne is most rewarding with food in a limited context, usually as an appetizer. Its acidity cuts through salt very well, so a partnership with caviar is perfect, and that same crispness makes it a good foil for smoked salmon; on a more commonplace level, for the same reason, it also matches with dips or spreads made with salt cod. It's one of the few wines that can pair with gravlax: salmon cured with sugar and salt, then usually served with a sprinkling of dill and a dab of honey-mustard sauce. In many ways, a Champagne brunch makes sense: Omelets, soufflés, corned beef hash, chicken hash, kedgeree, smoked sturgeon, and other white fish are all easily and comfortably eligible partners. At dinner, Champagne is traditionally served with a first course of fish mousse or quenelles, lifting their blandness nicely, unbothered by most of their usual reduced sauces. It's a wonderful revelation with many Chinese fish dishes, either Cantonese style (somewhat salty) or Szechwan (spicy hot). I could also make a good case for it with a basket of deep-fried calamari. Perhaps the best of all is sushi, where the succession of small dishes can become a string of perfect matches, thoroughly appetizing and appealing.

SHERRY

Dry sherry is not only one of the great wines of the world, it's half of one of the great food-and-wine tandems of the world, matching up with the savory small appetizers known as tapas in a gastronomic ritual that makes evenings in Spain unforgettable. There, you go into a bar and are confronted with glass cases or glass-covered dishes holding an array of small portions of foods: slices of dark-pink ham, sausages, various vegetables in sauces, meatballs, tiny fried fish or squid, fritters, several platters of olives, almonds, wedges of cold omelet, and whatever else the kitchen thinks might tempt you to stay and have another glass of chilled fino or manzanilla. It works, superbly.

- Champagne
- sherry
- chardonnay
- sauvignon blanc/fumé blanc
- semillon
- riesling
- pinot gris/grigio
- viognier
- soave
- albariño
- chenin blanc
- gewürztraminer
- rosé
- cabernet sauvignon
- merlot
- zinfandel
- pinot noir/ burgundy
- syrah/shiraz, and rhône-style blends
- barolo/barbaresco
- barbera
- chianti
- rioja
- dolcetto
- beaujolais/gamay
- valpolicella
- dessert wines

Dry sherry is white wine that is deliberately oxidized, and fortified with a bit of extra alcohol. In its first stages, a natural yeast grows on the wine while it's in barrels, which begins to create an aroma something like that of fresh bread; later, the wine is stored in a series of barrels that contain wine from previous years, in a three-step stage that deepens and fine-tunes the flavors as it matures. The final wine is bone-dry and strongly flavored, assertive but not heavy, with a slightly nutty aftertaste. A few decades ago, sweet sherries, usually labeled "cream sherry," were tremendously popular and confused a couple of generations of consumers as to what most sherry was really like, so now producers of dry versions call them by brand names, such as Tío Pepe, La Ina, and La Gitana. The first two are the most popular finos, and the latter is the best manzanilla, slightly fuller than fino; all three set the standard for what sherry ought to be.

Sherries are best enjoyed the Spanish way: as an appetizer, with snacks and nibbles like smoked clams, mussels, or oysters; with sausages (either spicy ones like chorizo or linguiça, or salami); baked stuffed mushrooms; ham croquettes; stir-fried or grilled prawns; olives; and almonds or cashews. With dinner, the traditional match has been with soup, such as consommé, but the best pairing is with gazpacho; dry sherry also goes well with salads combining fruit and nuts, such as pears, walnuts, and blue cheese. A good cross-cultural match is fino and tempura—the flavors of the various vegetables or fish as well as the crispness of the crusty batter and the taste of the soy-based sauce really suit the wine.

CHARDONNAY

Chardonnay is the most popular wine in the world. The grape is incredibly adaptable, and will grow almost anywhere. In a couple of places, where the soil and weather are poor enough to provide a real challenge, Chardonnay seems to accept the adversities as an exercise in character-building and responds by becoming great wine: In France, it happens in Champagne, and often in Chablis and along the "golden slope" of Burgundy where wines like Corton-Charlemagne, Meursault, and Puligny-Montrachet make connoisseurs around the world woozy with awe; it happens often enough in the Carneros

district of California and the cooler reaches of the Russian River Valley and other pockets around Sonoma, as well as in the fog-scoured canyons of Santa Barbara; recently, it's been found to occur on the high ridgelines of southern Australia, in the Adelaide Hills. In the international pecking order of dry white wines, these are the top guns. The reasons are relatively simple. The flavors of these cool customers are very, very definite, quite unmistakable, loaded with character—there is a balance of fruit, acidity, and texture that is immediately and quite obviously right, and despite the fact that these wines are never blended, there is complexity in the flavors, a persistence of their pleasures. Some are lean, some are fuller, but they all have that perfect balance in common.

The usual flavor association is with green apples like Granny Smiths, with overtones of figs or melons, and light touches of something like vanilla in the background. These are the wines for special occasions and rich food: lobster, any shellfish cooked or dunked in butter, oysters, sautéed scallops, Dover sole, roast sea bass, salmon prepared almost any way, bouillabaisse and other white fish stews like bourride (but not cioppino, as the acidity of the tomato sauce would get in the way), and the rich veal stew known as *blanquette de veau,* an old-fashioned, slightly decadent, and delicious dish.

The next level of Chardonnays is nothing to sneeze at, either; there's just a little less of that definiteness and persistent complexity, although there will still be a lovely balance and some authority in the flavor. Here are wines labeled with a wider geographic identity, such as simply Sonoma County or Santa Barbara County in California, and Columbia Valley in Washington state; from Australia, look for Adelaide Hills, Yarra Valley, and Margaret River; in France, well-known names of Chardonnay-based white Burgundies are Rully, Pouilly-Fuissé, St-Veran, and some Mâcon-Villages. These are wines for shellfish and full-flavored fish like flounder, bluefish, or swordfish, and barbecued or spicy blackened Cajun versions, as well as roast veal. They also have the muscularity to stand up to a classic Caesar salad.

From here on in, it's a matter of them being medium-bodied, pretty good white wines, with solid flavor and dryness but not a lot of complexity. These are usually labeled with the broadest of geographical definitions, like "California," "Southern Australia," various valleys in Chile, "Bourgogne" in France, and the names of several districts in Italy, for example. The first three exemplify what's considered the "New World" style, with fairly obvious fruitiness, fairly high alcohol, fuller body, and a lack of crispness that comes from low acidity, as well as a slight butterscotch aftertaste from oak flavorings; they're blunt, lacking in subtlety. The European versions at this level are leaner and less fruity, usually more acidic. On the whole, they're perfectly serviceable wines for a whole range of fairly simple preparations of poultry and fish, and come through on mixed-food occasions like buffets, where they can harmonize moderately well with a range of flavors.

SAUVIGNON BLANC/FUMÉ BLANC

Sauvignon Blanc is one of the most distinctive wines in the world, with a strikingly spicy, penetrating aroma, at once musky and tart; at its worst, it can have you wondering whether the family cat has been locked in the wine cellar too long. When it's balanced, however (and these days it is, most of the time), Sauvignon Blanc is crisp, refreshing, and lively, with a clear whistle of acidity running through it. It is also known as Fumé Blanc, from a slightly smoky aspect some people perceive when it's matured in oak barrels, which can give the wine some extra weight and fullness as it mellows. The grape reached its peak long ago in the Loire Valley of France, where it's named for the areas where it grows, such as Sancerre, Pouilly-Fumé, Quincy, or Ménétou-Salon; these have been the models for years: pure refreshment, absolute zest, a lovely lunchtime wine or pre-dinner drink, a perfect companion for freshwater fish from the Loire River like pike or perch, shad, and salmon, and a foil to cut through the butter that seems to go on everything there.

In this century, Sauvignon Blanc has traveled all over the world, and its accent has changed quite a bit wherever it's landed. In California, where it also picked up the alternative name of Fumé Blanc, the sunshine rather mellowed it out and the aroma became a little more floral, a model later followed by Washington state; in New Zealand, everything about it became more pronounced, even louder: The acidity cut deeper, the aroma was more pungent and herbal, and the body fuller, making it a wine strictly for those who loved its eccentric character (and, to be fair, there are a lot of those folks). In northeastern Italy, in the Adige Mountains, it is smooth and charming. In the rest of Italy, as in Bordeaux, Chile, Argentina, and eastern Europe, it has been just all right, with only a little individuality, basically unmemorable.

The best versions—for me, those are the ones from the Loire, California, Washington state, the Italian mountains, and about half the time New Zealand, in a good year—are fine pairings with food cooked with herbs, like fish with dill or oregano, or chicken with plenty of thyme. It makes a nice fit with lemongrass, ginger, and especially cilantro, so it's a good partner with Thai food and some Mexican dishes, and it's a real winner with a lot of Indian food, where it acts as a peacemaker to the clamor of spices. Best of all, it marries spectacularly well with garlic: Try it with chicken with forty cloves, or steamed bass or snapper stuffed with sliced garlic.

SEMILLON

Semillon is a fairly minor grape variety, but it's a very pleasant wine on its own and is often blended with Sauvignon Blanc to good effect, and it turns up in other blends as well, so this is a good place to mention it. On its own, as a dry wine, Semillon doesn't have much aroma; figs are the fruit it's compared with most often, and I can't remember what they smell like either. Nor does it have much acidity. It's pleasant, but the pleasures are fleeting. However (and it's a big however), well-made dry Semillon can age, and age well, evolving over the course of a decade or two into a medium-bodied, golden wine that has hints of honey and hazelnuts and a firm dryness, a wonderfully serious wine that tastes like no other. It happens with Semillons from the Hunter Valley in Australia, and sometimes with white Bordeaux from the Graves district, at least in good years. When they're young, well-made Semillons from Australia, Washington state, and Graves go well with oily fish like mackerel, shark, or mullet, especially when grilled over charcoal, but when they're aged, they're perfect with Mediterranean-style preparations of better fish: anything involving olive oil and lots of herbs, including bouillabaisse. Blended, they tame some of the pungency of Sauvignon Blanc, thereby improving it into a more versatile wine for drinking and serving with food. In some places where they don't have enough Chardonnay, like Australia, Semillon is used to stretch the wine, and usually known as "Semchard" or some similar variation, resulting in an average, decent jug wine.

RIESLING

Riesling is probably the most misunderstood wine in the world, mostly thanks to Germany, which has been producing great Riesling for centuries and not bothering to explain it very well to the rest of us. It is, by common consent, a noble wine, possessing some of the most delicious flavors any liquid has ever been blessed with; the confusion has arisen over the levels of sweetness, which the complicated German regulatory system has done little to clarify. As you really shouldn't miss out on something this wonderful, let me tell you just what you need to know:

First, make sure the label says Riesling. Forget Hock, ignore Liebfraumilch, then look for the term *Spätlese,* prominently displayed right above or below Riesling, which indicates a medium level of sweetness (usually well balanced by a vibrant zing of acidity). A bit of further insurance will be provided if the neck label bears a symbol of a silhouetted eagle clutching a bunch of grapes to its bosom, and the initials VDP; this is the sign of an organization of growers and wine makers using strict controls and procedures that aim for higher quality. The result is extraordinarily refreshing and lively, the ultimate match for cold, cracked Dungeness crab or lobster roll, and perfect with cold meat, like a roast beef sandwich or chicken. Its acidity and intrinsic richness makes it a good foil for sweetbreads, a similar light-but-rich food, and it also works well with cold, spicy dishes like Thai duck or beef salads. The rest of the Rieslings from Germany are indeed quite sweet, and quite wonderful too, but as they are dessert wines, I'll deal with them elsewhere.

Riesling is made in the rest of the world, mostly in a bone-dry style, but only the versions from Alsace and Australia are really worth seeking out. Alsatian Rieslings are their top wines, fairly high in alcohol (often 13 percent), with a nicely floral aroma and slightly austere crispness: serious wines, in other words, perfect with serious fish dishes like roast monkfish and salmon or grilled scallops, and with hearty pork stews or thick baked chops. Australian Rieslings are just as alcoholic, but their flavors tend to be leaner and the acidity more citric, almost lemony. They fall in the same flavor range as the Alsatians when it comes to food.

PINOT GRIS/GRIGIO

There's at least one Pinot Grigio on the menu of every Italian restaurant in the world, and with good reason: It's got well-developed pleasant flavors, and thus is Italy's most successful white wine. In the last decade, under its French name of Pinot Gris, it's also become Oregon's most successful white wine, so it's been turning up in a lot of other places too, which is good news. Pinot Gris isn't a terribly serious wine—it's light and lively and fresh, and has a faint smell and taste that remind me of apricots—but it's always a welcome one. In the Alsace region of France, it's a dry, above-average everyday wine, while in the northeastern mountains of Italy, just above Venice, it's just as popular as a fruitier, softer version. In Oregon, it falls somewhere between the two styles. It's amiable enough to be enjoyed on its own, and light enough to start a meal, good with pasta and pesto or cheese sauce or butter and herbs, or with light fish dishes.

(Another cousin in the Pinot family is Pinot Blanc, which is popular in Italy and turns up here and there around the world, valued mostly for its crisp acidity; it's often blended into sparkling wines for that reason. It's not worth seeking out, but if it comes your way, it's worth a try on the chance it may be above average.)

VIOGNIER

For centuries, Viognier has been grown successfully in a little patch in the mountains overlooking the Rhône River, where it produced one of the world's most expensive white table wines; elsewhere in France, it was finicky and difficult to grow, and nearly disappeared. In the last two decades, as red Rhône wines have become fashionable, some canny growers planted it in the warmer area along the southern coast of France, where it thrived and became the basis for humble *vins de pays*, "country wines" that are very much a bargain. California produces good versions, although the prices there are a bit exalted for what is essentially a low-acid, easygoing, aromatic wine (it smells lovely, like peach blossoms). Right now, though, it's the hottest new kid on the block.

Viognier is a good wine for aromatic, medium-flavored food, especially if it involves spices like nutmeg or cumin and cloves and Chinese five-spice powder, and dishes like roast chicken with herbs, old-fashioned chicken potpie, guinea fowl braised with red cabbage, roast pork, Cantonese-style roast pork or duck, lemon chicken, pasta salads with herbs and sausages, and North African stews that mix fruit, spices, and poultry in sweet-savory combinations.

SOAVE

Soave, made from a blend of native Italian grapes grown on the rolling hillsides near Verona, is a moderately delicate, amiable sort of wine that surprises you by the persistence of its lightly lemony flavors—it's got more finesse than you notice on the first sip. As none of the grapes in the blend make especially good wine anyplace else, it's bound to remain unique, a lovely drink that's perfect with freshwater fish, spaghetti with clam sauce, cold shrimp, or even boiled crab. The thing to look for is the appellation of Soave Classico, which means it came from the hills; simple Soave, grown on the plains below, can be too light and wispy, and not interesting for very long.

ALBARIÑO

Like Viognier, this is a newly fashionable wine, and very much so because the grape doesn't grow anywhere outside Spain and Portugal. The wines from Portugal, known as *vinhos verdes,* green wines, are often screamingly acidic and very much an acquired taste, but the Spanish versions, from the cool, windswept northwestern corner of the country, are lovely. They're still tart, but in a way that's merely refreshing, with a very clean aftertaste; they're considered to be Spain's best white wines, by far, and are terrific with Cajun-style seafood, spicy Mexican-style fish dishes like Pacific snapper with green peppers and onions, or shrimp in piquant sauce, and shellfish-and-chorizo combinations. They are also quite wonderful with pepperoni pizza.

CHENIN BLANC

Once upon a time, and a brief time it was, California Chenin Blanc was a pretty good food wine, in a useful, casual sort of way, fine for barbecues and picnics and cold chicken, but it got turned into a fairly sweet jug wine and lost its foothold. In France, in the Loire Valley, however, this grape can produce lovely, crisply vibrant wines. The best-known appellation there for Chenin Blanc is Vouvray, but Savennières is also very much worth seeking out; they're perfect partners for mussels steamed in white wine or steamed clams with drawn butter, or shellfish mousse. Sushi and dishes like calamari salad also marry well.

GEWÜRZTRAMINER

Gewürztraminer (pronounced with a hard g and accented on the second syllable–"guh-*vurts*") is the most distinctive of all wines, a wildly aromatic creature that fills the air around it with a mingling of exotic spices and mixed masses of wildflowers. When the grapes ripen in the vineyards, every bee within miles is drawn to their perfume, buzzing around in ecstasy (the harvesters hate it, and consider picking Gewürztraminer hazardous duty). It smells as if it's going to be sweet and fruity, but is often made bone-dry. Needless to say, it's an acquired taste. It's also a lovely one. The model is Alsatian, dry and fairly high in alcohol (about 13 percent), from northeastern France, where the diet is heavy with foie gras, roast pork, sauerkraut, heroic stews, and game. The fit is perfect.

For other diets, it's a tricky customer, although there's some synergy with spicy Hunan and Szechwan food. In California, the style is lighter all round, the alcohol lower, the aroma less pronounced, and the spiciness is balanced with a touch of sweetness that does no harm, either for casual drinking or with appetizers like prosciutto with melon, fried wontons dipped in plum sauce, rumaki, and fried calamari or clams.

ROSÉ

Pink wines are made from red grapes, the best of them echoing the flavor of what I think of as the parent grape; the color comes from the juice being in contact with the grape skins for a little while as it ferments, which also adds some flavor and character. The best-known pink wine is of course white Zinfandel, which is often denigrated by connoisseurs and sells millions of gallons every year anyway, a cheap and cheerful quaffing wine and often a pretty good companion to picnics and beach barbecues. Wines actually called rosé are usually more substantial and drier, often made from Zinfandel too, and they're a good match with a lot of Mexican, Indian, and Thai food, as are some French versions from the southern Rhône area, such as Tavel and Bandol. These dry versions are also absolutely the best wine for roast pork or grilled pork chops, having enough acidity to cut through the slight fattiness and enough fruity zing to liven up the blandly pleasant flavor of the meat. For a long

time, these sorts of wines, not entirely serious, have been denigrated by wine snobs as "compromise" wines when it comes to food pairings, which misses the point. Sure, they're compromises, but they also often work, which is good enough, and they do it with charm, which is even better.

CABERNET SAUVIGNON

This is the undisputed king of red wine grapes, responsible for many of the world's greatest, most long-lived wines. Unlike Chardonnay, which amiably adapts and assimilates itself to whatever climate and culture it finds itself in, Cabernet holds its own counsel, a bit aloof and somewhat stern, and altogether just a little grander than other red wines. Burgundies may be unbuttoned and sensuous, Rhônes sleeveless and carnal, but Cabernets always wear a tie and win arguments. That said, however, there is still a time when they're very good companions— when they're mature, they're a joy, obviously elegant, with expansive, deep, and lasting flavors. Drinking a fully mature fine Cabernet is like reaching the peak of a hill and seeing beautiful views for miles around. Right then, you know that whatever you've done to get to that point has been worth it, and you savor the moment. It's wonderful.

Cabernet is the major grape in most Bordeaux red wines, which tend to be blends with small amounts of other grapes (especially Merlot) included to add aroma, softness, spice, or fruitiness. When young, the wine can be a little rough and ungenerous, with mere hints of concentrated berry fruit in the flavor surrounded by dryly astringent tannin and vaguely herbal aromas; it seems unpromising stuff. Then, after five years or so, as it begins to soften, the discord fades, and the fruit is revealed. Over the next ten years, and often more, it just gets better all the time, becoming mellower, showing a variety of nuances of flavor, and retaining a refreshing acidity and persistence of those flavors.

Cabernet is grown in almost every country around the world with a temperate climate, and people debate the merits of those countries in an endless forum, often accompanied with comparative tastings and pseudo-scientific "evidence." Some of it's fun, especially when there are wine tastings involved. Generally, the top spots are conceded to a handful of great châteaus in

Bordeaux, with a small crowd of first-rate wineries in California coming along very closely, followed very, very closely by a small cluster of wineries in Australia, a handful in Washington, and a few in Italy. A little way down from the top, Chile comes into the picture, as do a couple of wines from Spain and one from Lebanon. It goes around like a spiral staircase, within and between countries and regions, descending through a whole hierarchy of levels, calculated by balances of fruit and acidity and the ability (or necessity) to age, by depth of flavor, by degrees of elegance and finesse. Price comes into it, too. This is also debated at length, making me wonder sometimes if the greatness of a wine isn't determined by how much people argue about it.

From the point of view of flavor, it can usually be said that the more expensive it is, the more concentrated it is, and therefore the longer you should wait to drink it; a $10 bottle of three-year-old Cabernet might be all right next Saturday night, but a $40 bottle would be more rewarding in three or four more years at least. When it comes to food matching, think concentration of flavor and texture: roast lamb or grilled thick lamb chops, charcoal-grilled steak, filet mignon, calf's liver with bacon and onions, and rich combinations like tournedos Rossini and others that combine foie gras and beef with hearty sauce. The tannin level of Cabernet, with its refreshing astringency, also makes it a good match with game, such as venison or squab, and the rich sauces that often accompany them.

MERLOT

Merlot is something of a chameleon among wines. It's generally an amiable sort of wine, easy to drink and good company for a variety of food, and relatively inexpensive to boot. Here and there, however, it's also one of the fine wines of the world, a sleek and elegant partner for epicurean food. Bordeaux's fabled Château Petrus is one example of those, as are a few dozen other Pomerols, and wines like the Napa Valley's Duckhorn and Shafer, Sonoma's Matanzas Creek, and Leonetti and Château Ste. Michelle from Washington state. At least, there's little possibility for confusion between the categories: The price tags for the latter group announce their intentions, loudly and clearly.

The good thing about most of the expensive Merlots is that, unlike Cabernet Sauvignon, they're fairly ready to drink at a young age, being softer and less harshly astringent—they won't dry out your mouth with tannin. This makes it the perfect solution if you're having an elegant dinner party and you don't have a wine cellar; shop around for a three- or four-year-old Merlot, and you'll be able to serve a fine wine with confidence. (And although it won't be cheap, it won't be as painful as buying a ten-year-old Cabernet or Barolo, assuming you can even find them.) The richness of these top Merlots makes them especially good partners for food like roast lamb or duck glazed with fruit sauce, and they're firm enough for a grilled steak.

The other 90 percent of the world's Merlots are fairly cheap and certainly cheerful, made to be drunk young, uncomplicated by oak flavors from expensive barrels. Their appeal lies in their straightforward fruit; it's a somewhat generalized flavor, not terribly distinctive, but quite appealing, easily earning its considerable popularity. The flavor leans toward plums, with a whisper of spice and a slight herbal tang in the aftertaste—in other words, it's easygoing, but with just enough complexity to stay interesting through a few refills of your glass. The levels of tannin and acidity are high enough to contribute some refreshment, but not obtrusive (Merlot is sometimes referred to by irreverent wine makers as "Cabernet without the pain," because of its low levels of astringent tannin).

Washington state and Chile make the most interesting inexpensive Merlots right now, in terms of dryness, character, and some ambitions to distinctiveness. California is right behind. Italian Merlot is notable mainly for its dryness, but lacks character; from the south of France, where it is labeled as Vin du Pays d'Oc and similar appellations of origin, the wine is extremely fruity, very plummy, and slightly sweet, better as a drink by itself, or maybe to accompany a casual barbecue.

Generally, these middle-of-the-road Merlots make a good match with everyday meals; they find a comfortable level with relatively simple straightforward foods with moderate acidity and a little spiciness, from meat loaf and Italian-style sausages to calf's liver with caramelized onions to North African–style meat dishes featuring cinnamon, cumin, and fruits, as well as traditional lamb stews made with carrots and other root vegetables that can give them a touch of sweetness. Some veal dishes with reduced sauces also work very well. It's also worth keeping in mind that this style of Merlot is a good fallback choice when you're economizing and still want to give yourself a treat. If wine were baseball, Merlot would be a reliable utility infielder with a batting average of just around .300—no shame in that at all.

ZINFANDEL

Zinfandel used to be known as "California's mystery grape," because it was obviously European, but no one really knew how it had arrived. Like a lot of immigrants, Zinfandel adapted and

acclimatized itself, worked hard, and paid its own way—at one point, it was the most widely planted red wine grape in California, although it got more respect for productivity than for finesse. When its ancestry was traced, things even looked a little worse—it comes from southern Italy and wasn't too highly regarded there either; its Italian name says it all: Primitivo.

All that has proved to be irrelevant. One of the things that distinguishes New World wine making from the European model is that in America and Australia and South America, there aren't layers upon layers of traditions and customs and rules that have to be rigidly adhered to. It's a double-edged sword, of course—some nontraditional American experiments, like pink Riesling or sweet Chardonnay, should have been used as drain cleaner instead of as a beverage—but basically it has liberated wine makers in these countries, and we've benefited from the alternative choices and variations. In the case of Zinfandel, there was even more of a clean slate, since there was no "family history" to get in the way, and the moderately ugly duckling turned into a swan as soon as it was treated with some respect.

Back then, in the early 1970s, most of the energy that transformed Zinfandel emanated from Sonoma and Amador Counties, where there were a lot of mature vineyards planted in the valleys and on the hillsides off the back roads. Old vines yield smaller crops, but the grapes have more concentrated and expressive and truer flavors, so these had all the potential to make fine, memorable wine. All they needed was to be treated the same way as the best Cabernets: careful harvesting, keeping grapes from individual vineyards in separate batches, controlling the fermentations, maturing the wines in oak barrels to deepen the flavors, and then blending only as much as necessary to bring out the best in the wine.

The marvelous thing about Zinfandel is that it's so alive with flavor when it's done right. The usual flavor association is with blackberries, and a good Zinfandel will usually taste like a handful of just-picked, fully ripe berries bursting in your mouth, extravagantly juicy, with a refreshing zing of acidity that keeps it lively. Most Zinfandels have fairly high alcohol and tannin (showing as a dark-purple inkiness), so they're rather strong when young, the sort of robust wine best suited to quite hearty food, like a venison stew or a dense beef-and-mushroom stew, or barbecued spareribs. There are also lighter versions (look for an alcohol reading on the label of less than 13 percent, and a color more like dark ruby red), where Zinfandel's unique combination of particular fruitiness and serious exuberance makes good matches for a variety of things like roast pork with gravy or rich sauce, osso buco, slow-braised lamb shanks, pasta with spicy sausages, and even first-rate cheeseburgers. When they're aged—and a ten-year-old Zin is often a thing of considerable beauty—they can turn out as well as any Cabernet, still lively but having gained some elegance, and can partner an elegant dinner with considerable grace.

PINOT NOIR/BURGUNDY

For a lot of connoisseurs, red Burgundy is the best wine of all, the absolute top of the list of all-time greats. Made in France from the Pinot Noir grape, the wine is unique, as it's light in color and body, with a delicate floral aroma that reminds some people of violets, yet it has an insistent, long-lasting richness of flavor that gains aristocratic elegance from a streak of vivacious acidity. The usual accolade is "an iron fist in a velvet glove." Because of that unique combination, Burgundy and good Pinot Noirs from elsewhere are perhaps the best all-round food wines, good partners with many preparations of fish, poultry, and meat.

The grape is finicky, a bit of a brat. It won't grow where it's too warm, or if the soil isn't just right, and it can be very difficult about ripening and then fermenting into wine. There is,

consequently, not enough of it to go around. In other words, good Burgundy is rare and thus expensive. California has had more success with it than most other areas: The Golden State has basically redefined many people's ideas of Pinot Noir, as the style there is fuller bodied and slighter rounder; there's still that combination of delicacy and power, but the wines are a bit more open. The Carneros region just north of San Francisco Bay has the edge, but Sonoma, Santa Barbara, San Luis Obispo, Anderson Valley in Mendocino, and a few other places where the Pacific fog can creep in and cool things off do well too. Oregon has also made a name for Pinot Noir, and in good vintages—about half the time—is well worth seeking out. More and more, Australian and New Zealand wine makers are also turning out interesting Pinot Noirs, different from Burgundy, but similar enough to recognize.

The flavor association most often invoked is with thoroughly ripe black cherries, and the tannin in Pinot Noir is soft enough to give the wine a velvety texture. The aroma is another matter. Most Burgundies and Pinot Noirs, even the great ones, have a whiff of what we call "barnyard," which is a euphemism for a light smell of manure—not sulphurous or nasty, but slightly funky. Pour a glass and expose the wine to air, and it begins to fade, but it can be a surprise; just be aware that it's not a flaw. Because of the prominent cherryish fruit and the smoothness, the classic combination is with roast beef, especially when the meat is carved in the thick slices that give it a similar texture. Roast salmon is another classic combination. I like it a lot with quail, which is mostly slightly dark meat, and with roast turkey, and duck. The gamey quality in the aroma, and the touch of earthiness in many Pinot Noirs, also make it a good match with dishes featuring mushrooms, like mushroom risotto, or beef with a morel sauce. Best of all is beef stew, the classic long-simmered, deeply flavored *boeuf à la bourguignonne*, made with chunks of well-marbled chuck steak, carrots, onions, and red wine; it's a perfect marriage of food and wine, the definition of *synergy*.

SYRAH/SHIRAZ, AND RHÔNE-STYLE BLENDS

The Rhône River flows over five hundred miles, tumbling from the Swiss Alps into France and then down into the Mediterranean just west of Marseilles. It's been a principal thoroughfare since Roman times, and the steep, terraced hillsides of its long valley have been planted in grapevines for almost a thousand years. In the Middle Ages, the local wine became famous when Pope Clement V moved the papal court and entourage to Avignon (which is why the most famous wine of the area became Châteauneuf-du-Pape, named for the estate near the "new house of the Pope"). Even when the court moved back to Rome, Rhône vineyards still provided the house wine.

Given the length of the valley, it's hardly surprising that the red wines of the Rhône reflect a diversity of climate, between the cool northern end and the quite warm south, of raw material (the wines of the north are made from Syrah, the wines of the south are blends of several grapes), and a considerable difference in style and approachability—the wines of the north can be somewhat austere and ungenerous when young, requiring several years of aging to get to an easier maturity, while the wines of the south are generous and voluptuous, reflecting the sunshine from the edges of neighboring Provence. All the grapes involved in both places have traveled widely and make fascinating wines elsewhere in the world, and are sometimes lumped together as if they were the same, so I'll discuss them separately.

The Rhône version of Syrah is generally considered to be some-what noble, as if it were the cousin of aristocrats. Its reputation is mainly based on the fact that the wine can age well, evolving, over a decade or two, from being as hard and tight as a fist to open-handed warmth, while retaining some seriousness and weight. Unlike some of the noble red varieties, its virtue doesn't come from having complex or multifaceted flavors, but from its fullness and the persistence of its dark-berry-and-spice flavor: A fifteen-year-old Hermitage or Côte Rôtie will hit a high top note of taste at the first sip, and stay up there to the end of the bottle. As a partner, it will dance with every red meat in the room, but be most lively with the spicy ones, like steak *au poivre* or venison with any of the usual dense sauces, Mexican beef dishes like

carne asada, and duck curry. Other appellations to look for from the northern Rhône are Cornas, Crozes-Hermitage, and St-Joseph, which tend to be lighter and easier to drink when young, say at four or five years old.

Elsewhere in the world, Syrah has been something of a hostage to fortune. It does well, and hangs on to the best attributes of its Rhône cousins, in California and Washington state, although the wine-making style in those places emphasizes the berryish fruit and tones down the tannin, so that it's a luscious drink fairly young. One Italian winery, Isole e Olena in Tuscany, makes a terrific version, which some other Italians are emulating.

There is a lot of Syrah in Australia, where it's a leading variety, known there as Shiraz. It makes a fairly wild wine there, almost feral: It can be aggressively funky, with overtones of leather or black licorice in the aroma and flavor (the Aussies used to brag about that aspect, saying the wine should smell like a sweaty saddle). There are some lighter and smoother versions, but Shiraz is definitely an acquired taste; even when it's blended with other varieties (and Australian wine makers will blend anything they feel like with Shiraz, to the point of complete flavor anarchy), that tangy funk can come through, loud and all too clear, only fading with considerable age, like twenty or so years. As far as food matching goes, I don't think I'd want to run into whatever goes with most Shiraz, either on a plate or late at night out in the woods.

The wines of the southern Rhône are very different, more easygoing than those of the north. Down there, the countryside is smoother and the climate warmer, and it shows in the wines, which tend to be amiable, softer, and easier to drink when young. Here, they are blends of Grenache, Syrah, and several other varieties, slightly high in alcohol (more than 13 percent) but also jam-packed with lush fruit that offsets it, and only moderate in acid. They're voluptuous and big, but fleshy rather than muscular, with an aroma that jumps out of the glass. Syrah is often in the mix also, to provide some firmness and an ability to age. There are some very good, above-average wines made here, and some outstanding good-value wines too. Wines from Châteauneuf-du-Pape are certainly worth seeking out, especially the fabled wines of Beaucastel and Vieux Télégraphe, as are those from the areas of Gigondas and Vacqueyras. A lot of bargains can be found among the group known as Côtes-du-Rhône Villages, which are generally slightly lighter than the top wines. Wines labeled simply Côtes-du-Rhône are a large, looser category: They are what's left over. They're always worth trying, at least, though they tend to be pretty ordinary.

Elsewhere, I'd say California has come out best in emulating these wines. There is an increasing amount of Syrah around, in Napa and the Carneros district of Sonoma, and even in Santa Barbara, producing quite elegant, serious wine that more than holds its own against the French competition. Also, a while back, a group of young wine makers, who called themselves the "Rhône Rangers," discovered that a lot of old California vineyards were planted in several of the same grape varieties that flourish in the southern Rhône (often under different names from those in France). They've done a terrific job of producing the same sort of lush, rich, amiable wines. Australia is the other major competitor, with their blends of Shiraz, Grenache, Mataro, and other grapes (in Australia, all the grapes in a blend are listed on the label). Some are terrific and some are rough and raspy—definitely taste before you buy.

North or south, Rhône or California or Washington, these are wines for food. The directness and richness of Syrah-based wines, well aged, make them perfect with grilled steak or beef stew and casseroles, grilled lamb chops and lamb stew, and venison. The southern blends are more adaptable, their softer richness making them perfect with *cassoulet,* grilled stuffed eggplant, thick slabs of tuna simmered in chopped tomatoes and onion, or even grilled tuna steaks, sautéed calf's liver and onions, roast duck, rich tomato-and-cheese pizza or calzone, and barbecued chicken.

BAROLO/BARBARESCO

In Italy, they call Barolo "the king of wines, the wine of kings," and the hype isn't far off the mark. It's certainly a wine rich in flavor, in cultural associations, and also in history: Thomas Jefferson, America's first international wine-lover, was a fan of the wine more than two hundred years ago, and he was followed by a long line of European nobility. What's unusual about it,

however, is that quite a few ordinary wines are made from the same grape, known as Nebbiolo; the thing that matters most in the mountains of northwestern Italy is where it's from. Upper-class here really means *up,* and the slopes are steep, too—inspecting a famous vineyard here is an invitation to vertigo. Luckily, we don't have to learn any geography or memorize a lot of tedious classification systems to know who's in the top ranks, as only the best vineyards are entitled to use the names of Barolo and Barbaresco, which are the two hilly districts in the Piedmont region that produce this extraordinary, rich, and forceful wine (Barbaresco is the slightly lighter version). Everything else made from Nebbiolo has to be called something else, and at best they're just average.

Barolo and Barbaresco are full-bodied and robust but elegant wines, with complex aromas of dried flowers, a hint of tar, a flash of some earthiness like mushrooms; the flirtation here is serious, a little libertine. They need at least ten years after the vintage to come around to maturity, and during that time they just get more complex, evolving into one of the world's best red wines. They are wines for special occasions, best with beef, especially something as rich as pot roast or beef braised in red wine, oxtail stew, osso buco, and roast lamb.

BARBERA

Barbera is one of Italy's workhorse grapes, growing everywhere, producing reliable, sturdy, and fairly rustic full-bodied wines, the sort that everyone takes for granted as everyday house wines, useful and pleasant enough but nothing special. At one time, they were also fairly low in tannin, which meant that they were moderately light and wouldn't age—wines of the moment. However, up in the northwest corner of Italy, in the cool and mountainous area of the Piedmont, Barbera was often a bit better than that average, with a little bit more snap, some more vibrancy, some more muscle, in a way. Some young wine makers got the idea that they could elevate its status and make it more consistently flavorful if they matured it in new oak barrels, the reason being that oak adds its own tannins to wine, makes it firmer, and helps it age better. The difference between the new style and the old was very much night and day, and today Barbera from the Piedmont commands respect. It's also more expensive, of course, but still pretty good value. Elsewhere in the world, including (sadly) California, Barbera is mostly grown as a blending variety, to add color and acidity to everyday wines: an unsung hero if there ever was one.

The flavor when young is direct and savory, with its lively acidity ricocheting around your mouth, fairly fruity and quite dry; it's not complex, but not monotonous either. After three or four years, the dryness eases a little and it seems a bit fuller, but still vibrant. It's a wine for Italian-style food, with a richness the wine can cut through or play off: anything with meat, tomatoes, and onions; sausages with pasta or lentils; lamb-and-bean stew; braised duck; and chicken livers any style, but especially chicken-liver risotto.

CHIANTI

Chianti is a regional name; the wine is a blend of different grapes. It is probably one of the most familiar wine names in the world, but until recently Chianti was usually underrated, probably because not enough people were aware that it's been going through a vivid renaissance over the past decade, a creative surge that followed a long overhaul of the vineyards and an expensive modernization in the wineries of Tuscany.

Chianti has been made for more than five hundred years, and everything about it was tired by the 1970s. It took almost twenty years for enterprising young wine makers to change the system and throw out the old traditions that were holding them back. Now, the new generation of wines from Chianti are a revelation, fresh, lively, very dry, and lightly savory, and fitting into a useful middle-weight range of body and strength. They can age well, but don't necessarily need to, so you can enjoy a three-year-old bottle as well as a five- or six-year-old one. It's not terribly complex wine, but the best of them have a kind of rustic elegance, good with lighter meats without rich sauces, such as rabbit, casseroled pheasant or guinea hen, roast pork or grilled thick pork or veal chops, and sautéed calf's liver with caramelized onions.

Chianti is made mostly from the Sangiovese grape, and there are quite a few Californians who have transplanted it and are making a similar wine under the varietal name, so far in small batches, but it's definitely worth trying, although the Italians may be better value right now.

RIOJA

Over the last twenty years, Spain has catapulted itself into the modern world of wine making, and Rioja, where the best wines come from, has led the way. The wine is a blend of Tempranillo, which has a lovely aroma like violets and tastes so fruity it's almost sweet; Grenache, which gives it a boost of alcohol and helps it age; and a bit of a few other varieties that provide complexity. Some Riojas are released a year after the vintage (the label will announce it as *joven,* a youth), but most are matured in small barrels made of American oak, which gives the wine a slight touch of flavor and aroma that's like vanilla, then aged in the bottle; Rioja *reserva* isn't released until the wine is at least four years old, and *gran reserva,* made only in very good years, comes out when it's six or more. Both can age further, for several more years. Maybe because of all these unique aspects, Rioja stands alone, and that may be why it lacks snob appeal, which also means it doesn't command the prices it deserves—good news for those of us who appreciate good value.

Rioja is a fine match with lamb, especially slow-simmered lamb shanks and rich stews, and dark-meat birds like pigeon, duck, and pheasant; beef or liver with well-cooked onions also works well, as the wine and onions echo each other's hints of almost sweetness. For the same reason, barbecued pork is also a winner with it.

DOLCETTO

Dolcetto is the name of the grape as well as the wine in northwestern Italy, in the Piedmont region, where it's the everyday, easygoing choice for meals or a few glasses among friends. It's basically an uncomplicated wine, fairly soft and quite dry, reminiscent of bittersweet small-berry fruits like mulberries. It's a good wine year-round, gently warming in winter and refreshing in summer (being soft, it gains a little snap when chilled).

Dolcetto is a good partner for pasta with cheese sauce or vegetables, either warm or as a salad, or stuffed, as in ravioli. It's also very good with cheese fondue, quiche, salade niçoise, roast Cornish hen, and any of the various chicken dishes sautéed with tomatoes, onion, garlic, and other vegetables.

BEAUJOLAIS/GAMAY

Beaujolais is the region to the south of Burgundy, warmer and with a gentler landscape, often thought of as the simpler sibling of the noble Burgundy, somewhat the less-ambitious kid brother. There's more than a bit of truth in that, but the fact is that good Beaujolais is one of the most amiable and useful wines there is: Being fairly soft but fruity in a plummy sort of way, it's a very pleasant drink, and it's got enough fullness and follow-through to be a good match for quite a lot of different food. The image problem probably arises from the hype surrounding the annual madness when the just-made, barely fermented "Nouveau" Beaujolais is released just after the harvest, usually late in November, and rushed to market all over the world in a hoopla of races and contests dreamed up by some marketing guys a few decades ago, and sort of fun in a brain-dead way. "Who will be first to drink it?" they ask. "Who cares?" real wine-lovers reply, "Nouveau is just grape juice on steroids."

The standard versions are basically meant for refreshment, not reflecting on. There are essentially two groups of worthwhile Beaujolais: Wines labeled as Beaujolais-Villages tend to be light and refreshing, not terribly acidic, straightforwardly grapey, informal, and one-dimensional beverages meant to be drunk a year or two after the harvest. They're lightweight enough to go with a picnic or a fairly broad weekend-brunch menu, and are fine lightly chilled. The more serious Beaujolais carry the names of actual villages on the labels: Fleurie, Moulin-à-Vent, Morgon, Chiroubles, St-Amour, Juliénas, Chénas, Côtes de Brouilly, and Brouilly. They're well worth looking out for, as they're some of the most appealing wines around, with lovely, heady aromas, persistent flavor that isn't diminished just because it's uncomplicated, and just enough concentration to make a good match with well-flavored, somewhat rustic food, like shepherd's pie or meat loaf or

Danish-style meatballs in cream sauce, and other comfort foods. It's also good with pork or chicken, and comfortable with old-fashioned pan gravy (as opposed to intense reduced sauces).

There are also a few wines labeled Gamay from California. The grape is actually a different one, due to some confusion long ago, but it's made in a similar light, refreshing style and is a worthwhile wine in the same way as the village wines.

VALPOLICELLA

Also often good value because of a past image problem is Valpolicella, which is a light blend of grapes from the region above Verona in northern Italy. For a long time, the vines were pushed to produce too many grapes and made into wine in

industrial quantities; they were cheap, and deservedly so. The modern generation of wine makers has turned the situation around, however, and Valpolicella from the hillsides (labeled as Valpolicella Classico) is an appealing choice when you want a light red; it has a red-cherry fruitiness, a lively acidity, and a tangy dryness—very refreshing, perfect with rich vegetable dishes like pumpkin or red-pepper risotto and stuffed eggplant, quiches, roast loin of veal, grilled chicken, and ham. It also tastes good lightly chilled, and is a nice match that way with chicken-liver pâté for an offbeat first course for a hearty dinner.

DESSERT WINES

Whatever its gastronomic levels and aspirations, every wine-producing country makes sweet wines, even when doing so isn't easy—in fact, the ingenuity employed to indulge the world's sugary cravings has been quite extraordinary in many instances.

These days, we can avail ourselves of all the world's surviving fads, notions, and follies; there's no shortage of choice in the bustling American marketplace. A good place to try unfamiliar dessert wines is in restaurants that offer them by the glass. At home, the choices are nearly unlimited, depending on your approach to desserts in general. The simple approach makes the wine the soloist: An old vintage port, say, is served with blue cheese and walnuts or almonds, or an intensely sweet, golden late-harvest Sauternes might be matched with vanilla-almond cookies or a slice of apple tart. The other, more dramatic approach would be more along the lines of a grand-finale duet, serving the port with a death-by-chocolate cake or a densely rich mince pie, while the Sauternes might join a caramelized pear tart or a wedge of filo-almond-honey pastry.

The basic limitations on matching desserts and wine are defined by some aspects of the foods, such as temperature and texture: Frozen desserts like ice cream dull the palate and crowd out any other flavors, for example, while soft custards coat the tongue and don't let other flavors in. Acidity, as in fruit salads, can throw the flavor of the wine off. A good rule of thumb is to choose a dessert that's slightly less sweet than the wine. Otherwise, the usual idea prevails: Balance is all.

The most robust and full-bodied dessert wine is port, which comes in vintage and nonvintage versions, as well as a few curiosities in between, such as "late-bottled vintage" and "vintage character," which attempt to create a few more marketing niches between the basic, fairly cheap type, and the vintage, fairly expensive type. The distinctions are shown by the prices, and they're actually useful: Join in the game where you can afford the admission. Port goes well with bittersweet chocolate, whether plain or in cakes or tarts (but not milk chocolate, which just clogs up your palate). It's quite good with plum pudding and really sensational with mince pie, which makes it a good bet as a

holiday closer at Thanksgiving and Christmas. The traditional notion of blue cheese and walnuts is also a very good one. Another version of port that's sometimes overlooked is tawny port, which has a lovely amber color, less sweetness, and more mellow roundness than the ruby types. Rather than being vintage dated, tawny ports are usually labeled by the amount of time they've been matured in large oak casks: "10-year-old," "20-year-old," and so on. They're also winners at holiday time, as there is nothing better with pumpkin pie.

The rarest and most expensive of all dessert wines is Sauternes, the golden, richly sweet wine of southern Bordeaux. It tastes of honey, with a tinge of apricot, and has a concentrated, luscious fullness of body—it feels as luxurious as it is. Sauternes is the best example of a group of "late-harvested" wines, which are made from grapes left on the vines long after all the other grapes have been picked, usually well into October, or sometimes even November. The grapes shrivel in the autumn sun, and the evaporation concentrates their sugar; they look like moldy raisins by the time they're picked. The wines they make are terrifically sweet, but are also given a lift by a taut current of underlying acidity (which helps the wines to age for a long time—it's not uncommon to see ten- and twenty-year-old Sauternes for sale). The other notable wine in this category is German, made from Riesling, and known as "Trockenbeerenauslese," meaning "dried grapes selectively picked" (usually in small clusters, by hand). The grape is different from those in Bordeaux, but the late-harvest process provides a similar character to the wine. There is also a late-harvested Hungarian wine, known as Tokay, that is very like these in flavor.

The most offbeat dessert-wine types are those made from the Muscat family of grapes, whose spicy and faintly but pleasantly musky aroma and flavor are unmistakable: The distinctive note survives whatever's done in the wine making, ringing out in full-bodied, fortified port-type wines from Australia, light white French ones, and a couple of offbeat oddities from California, and then sounding a gentle chime in the sparkling Asti Spumante from Italy. The spiciness makes these wines tricky for anything but simple desserts, but they're very pleasant matched with polenta cake with almonds, or nut-rich cookies like Italian biscotti. It's best to think of dessert wines as divas—they're the stars.

A WORLD OF FOOD

Here are recipes for wine-friendly dishes, classic and contemporary, with specific or multiple wine choices for each, as well as some general principles for making perfect matches. Some wines are distributed on a limited basis, so it's impossible to recommend brands, but this generic approach will put you in a specific flavor zone, at least. Obviously, your own taste is the final arbiter: You may find New Zealand Sauvignon Blanc too strong and acidic but think California Sauvignon Blanc is just right, really refreshing, and that will become your choice, which is what it's all about, in the end.

I've included European wines among the recommended matches mostly on the basis of similarities: in many cases, the same grapes are used (that is, Chablis is made from Chardonnay, red Burgundy from Pinot Noir); in some cases, the similarities are of the basic characteristics of the wines: lightness, or acidic crispness, or robust power, and the like. As we in America have access to all the best wines of the world, it's silly not to make the most of those choices.

APPETIZERS

In most countries, appetizers are an integral part of the cultural ritual, bits of food that go with the wine and fuel the everyday socializing, gossip, and cheerful byplay of life. Around the eastern Mediterranean, especially in Greece and Turkey, they're *mezze,* in Spain *tapas,* in Russia *zakuski,* in Italy *antipasti:* savory, often ingenious snacks eaten without cutlery or ceremony as you ease into the evening. The French formalized their *hors d'oeuvre* by integrating them into dinner, and the English took that idea even further with luxurious delicacies served from elaborate trolleys and silver trays. In our complicated American medley, echoing so many of these gastronomic tunes, it often seems that the melody has gotten a bit lost. Certainly, we can all do better than the usual "glass of white wine" that often doesn't go well with any of the snacks on offer.

For many of us in the wine business, the best wake-up call for the palate is *fino,* the light, dry sherry from southern Spain; it matches extremely well with all sorts of foods, from smoked salmon and other smoked fish to several kinds of sausages, and olives and nuts—just about everything but caviar (they flatten each other). Champagne is the usual choice for many people, as much for its celebratory aspect and luxuriousness as for flavor, and its acidity and sparkle take it a long way with most foods, except for strong cheeses and cheese-based dips. (A nice, inexpensive alternative bubbly is Prosecco, the light, refreshing sparkling wine from northern Italy.)

White wine is indeed better than red as a starter, mostly because of its lightness, higher acidity, and lower tannins; it simply makes an easier accommodation with a range of foods, and is generally more refreshing. It's worth planning which white to offer, though. If there are a lot of salty snacks or smoked fish, a fruity wine like a first-rate German Riesling, which has good underlying acidity, should be perfect. Pinot Gris, with its apricot-fruit overtones and pleasant aroma, is also very versatile. Often the white wine of choice is everybody's favorite, Chardonnay, but between its high alcohol and the touches of smoky oak in its pronounced flavor, it's not always successful.

Looking at it from the food side, almost anything goes, although avoiding extremes of flavor helps the interplay. Unsalted nuts are better than salted; chilies should be used sparingly; vinegar-based sauces flatten wine; and strongly flavored vegetables can make some wines taste odd (for example, raw turnips or celery with some cheese dips). For the most part, though, this side of the food-and-wine equation is especially easy—and pleasant.

GRUYÈRE CHEESE PUFFS

These are popular snacks in Burgundy, and are featured at wine tastings hosted by wine merchants, for the simple reasons that they're irresistible and delicious, and make any white wine and most light reds taste better.

{wine recommendation: pinot noir}

1 CUP WATER

½ TEASPOON SALT

½ CUP (1 stick) UNSALTED BUTTER

1 CUP ALL-PURPOSE FLOUR

4 EGGS, LIGHTLY BEATEN

1 CUP (4 ounces) SHREDDED GRUYÈRE CHEESE

Makes about eighteen puffs

~Line a baking sheet with parchment paper.

~Preheat the oven to 400°F.

~In a medium, heavy saucepan, combine the water, salt, and butter. Bring the water to a boil over medium-high heat. As soon as the butter melts, stir in the flour all at once. Reduce the heat to low and stir vigorously until the dough begins to come away from the sides of the pan. Remove from heat and stir in the eggs a little at a time; the dough will thicken and become shiny. Stir in the cheese vigorously, beating in some air.

~Spoon teaspoonfuls of the dough 1 inch apart onto the prepared pan. Bake for 20 to 25 minutes, or until lightly browned. Remove the pan from the oven and transfer the puffs to wire racks to cool briefly. Serve warm.

SESAME BLUE-CHEESE SAVORIES

I like to have something ready that will be immediately satisfying when people arrive for lunch or dinner, something light but savory. These little cookies did the job for me when I was a guest at a country-house hotel, so I wheedled the recipe out of the chef, Shaun Hill, now chef-owner of his own restaurant, the Merchant House, in the little town of Ludlow, which is famous for having more Michelin-starred restaurants than any city in England outside of London. Any fruity white wine will match up well.

{wine recommendation: riesling, pinot gris}

1¼ CUPS SELF-RISING FLOUR

¾ CUP (1½ sticks) COLD UNSALTED BUTTER, CUT INTO 1-INCH CHUNKS

4 OUNCES BLUE CHEESE, CRUMBLED (about ⅞ cup)

¼ CUP SESAME SEEDS

Makes about twenty savories

~Spread the flour on a work surface. Roll the chunks of butter in the flour by hand, breaking them up as you do, until it's a mixture of small lumps and crumbs, the flour thoroughly mixed in. Sprinkle the cheese over and roll again to mix in the cheese, then form into a ball. Wrap in plastic wrap and refrigerate for at least 2 hours, or up to 4 hours.

~Preheat the oven to 450°F. On a lightly floured surface, roll the dough out to a ¼-inch thickness. Cut into any shape you want—strips, squares, small balls—no more than 1 inch in size. Roll or pat them in the sesame seeds. Place on a baking sheet at least 1 inch apart (they'll expand) and bake until slightly browned, 12 to 14 minutes. Remove from the oven. Transfer to wire racks to cool.

Note: Self-rising flour is merely flour that has had baking powder and salt added—it makes this simple recipe even easier.

SWEET ONION–PECAN PIZZETTE

This appetizer was created to go with just about any light white wine. It's based on a staple snack in Provence, known as *pissaladière,* the French version of pizza, which is topped with onion, anchovies, and black olives—delicious, and wonderful with the local red wine, but fairly salty and pungent. This recipe keeps the richly sweet onion topping, but garnishes it with pecans, whose subtle flavor and crunch complement the onions perfectly.

{ wine recommendation: viognier, sauvignon blanc }

4 TABLESPOONS OLIVE OIL

1 POUND ONIONS, FINELY CHOPPED

8 OUNCES PIZZA DOUGH

1 TEASPOON DRIED THYME

1 CUP (4 ounces) PECAN HALVES

Makes thirty-six pieces

~In a large, heavy saucepan, heat 2 tablespoons of the olive oil over medium-high heat. Add the onions, stir well, and reduce heat to low; the onions should cook very slowly without coloring at first. Cook for 45 minutes, or until they're quite mushy—it will seem as if nothing much is happening except that your kitchen smells increasingly good for the first 30 minutes, and then they'll begin to brown nicely.

~Preheat the oven to 450°F. On a lightly floured surface, roll the dough out into a 12-inch square about 1/4 inch thick. Transfer to a lightly oiled heavy baking sheet. Brush the top of the dough liberally with the remaining 2 tablespoons olive oil and sprinkle the thyme over it. Spread the onions over in a layer. Place the pecan halves in rows about 2 inches apart. Bake for 15 to 20 minutes, or until a deep golden color. Remove from the oven. Let cool to room temperature, about 30 minutes. Cut into 2-inch squares between the pecans and serve.

BRANDADE DE MORUE

Salt cod is wonderful to eat and easy to make. Don't wander off, now—this could change your life in small but very pleasant ways. Fish cured in salt wouldn't be so popular all over the world if it weren't pretty good stuff, and salt cod is the best of those. I was won over when I visited a wine maker in Spain and was served a hot slice of toasted bread liberally smeared with a delicious garlicky puree that he called *brandada de bacalao*. A day later, in Boqueria, the extraordinary covered market in Barcelona, I noticed stacks of white bricks on several tables: salt cod, though it looked like sugar-frosted white chocolate. Unable to resist, I brought some home in my luggage (no problem—it's odorless).

Salting is a common form of curing, as in ham or corned beef, but in fish it tends to be less obvious, at least in its final form (it's not really very salty), and it does wonders for the texture. Lately, I've been doing my own, and the results are even better, and a lot cheaper.

Here's how: Fill a shallow oval or rectangular dish (I use a glass baking dish) with 1/2 inch of kosher salt, place a fillet of cod on top of it, and pour more kosher salt over, burying the fish. Cover with plastic wrap and refrigerate for 1 week. The salt will form a crust and then a kind of slurry as it draws the water out of the fish, which will shrink a little and firm up. Remove from the dish, discard the salt, rinse the fish and the dish, and put the fish back in the fridge, immersed in cold water; change the water 2 or 3 times a day for 2 days, and then you're ready to use it. This method also works well for any flaky fish: Haddock is quite good, for example, and it restores many fish that are usually sold previously frozen, like orange roughy.

Brandade de morue (the French name) is a classic dish, good on its own and as the base for many dips and spreads. The traditional version is a terrific match for acidic whites with some muscle and attitude, and even for really dry Riesling from Alsace or Australia. Brandade is usually served warm, with crackers or slices of toasted baguettes. You could also make a more elegant presentation by spreading some on toasted baguettes, topping them with shredded Gruyère or grated Parmesan cheese, and running them under a broiler until the cheese browns.

{wine recommendation: sauvignon blanc, albariño}

1 SALT COD, RINSED

1/4 CUP EXTRA-VIRGIN OLIVE OIL

1/2 CUP MILK AT ROOM TEMPERATURE

2 CLOVES GARLIC, COARSELY CHOPPED

1/4 TEASPOON GROUND WHITE PEPPER

1 TEASPOON FRESH LEMON JUICE

1 POTATO, PEELED, SLICED, AND BOILED (optional)

~In a medium saucepan, bring 2 cups of water to a boil. Add the fish and turn off the heat; let cool. Drain the fish, then flake it roughly by hand, feeling for small bones as you do. In a blender or food processor, combine the fish and all the remaining ingredients. Process until quite smooth. If it seems slightly stiff, add a little more oil and milk, 1 teaspoon of each at a time. The potato is up to you; it's not traditional, but increasingly common, and it makes the mixture smoother.

A QUARTET OF BRUSCHETTAS

There's one dish that is nearly universal all around the European side of the Mediterranean: bread toasted over a fire, rubbed with garlic, and sprinkled with sea salt and olive oil. In much of Italy, it's called *bruschetta,* but in Tuscany it's *fettunta,* in Greece *khoriatico,* and in most of Spain *pa amb oli.* In Barcelona, street vendors pile tomato pulp on it, and on the southern coast, it's not complete without a grilled sardine on top. It may seem to be the simplest of foods, but it inspires quite extended conversations around kitchen tables in those countries: how much garlic you rub in, which oil is best, to salt or not, and so on. Then, when the talk gets around to toppings and garnishes, it really gets intense, and you realize this isn't peasant food anymore.

This is one time when Americans, especially on the West Coast, have an edge, because sourdough bread is simply the best base for good bruschetta. Ciabatta isn't bad, and any unsalted, rough-textured country-French-style loaf is good, too. Traditionally, it is made from day-old bread sliced ½ inch thick, but for entertaining, I find that sourdough baguettes cut on a sharp diagonal and allowed to sit out for an hour or so (to dry out and make a crisp bruschetta) work well.

They're best toasted by flame, on an outdoor grill or under the broiler, rubbed lightly with a halved clove of garlic while they're still quite warm, and drizzled or brushed with extra-virgin olive oil. If they're going to be eaten plain, sprinkling them with a pinch of sea salt makes them taste better;

otherwise, salt is optional. Toppings should be spooned on, but not neatly spread—this isn't an open-faced sandwich. I like to make a couple of toppings and hand them around in bowls with the toasted bread, to let people make their own choices. Here are four of my favorites.

Note: each recipe makes about twelve bruschettas

CONTINUED

BRUSCHETTA WITH BRANDADE AND GREEN PEPPERS

This one is from Abruzzo, on Italy's east coast, which is known for quite rustic food and fairly nondescript white wine. With more options available to us, we can make a better match with a white that's lightly fruity, refreshing, and very dry.

⊰ wine recommendation: verdicchio, pinot grigio, oregon pinot gris ⊱

8 OUNCES SALT COD

1 POUND GREEN BELL PEPPERS, ROASTED AND PEELED (see note)

2 TABLESPOONS OLIVE OIL

4 SPRIGS THYME

1/2 TEASPOON RED PEPPER FLAKES

2 CLOVES GARLIC

1 TABLESPOON CAPERS, DRAINED

~Blanch cod as described on page 60, cool, and flake. Cut the peppers into strips. In a heavy skillet over medium heat, heat the olive oil and sauté the peppers, thyme, red pepper flakes, and garlic for about 10 minutes. Discard the thyme and slice the garlic. Place the peppers on a cutting board. Scatter the garlic, cod, and capers on top of the peppers and coarsely chop everything together with a heavy knife, mixing as you go. The mixture should be thoroughly amalgamated but still a bit chunky. Put it in a glass bowl and refrigerate overnight, to let the flavor develop.

Note: Roasting and peeling peppers: Preheat the broiler. Cut the peppers in half. Remove the seeds and ribs. Broil until well charred. Place in a paper bag, close, and let cool for 15 minutes. Rub off the skin.

TUSCAN BRUSCHETTA WITH TUNA AND CANNELLINI

Many bruschetta toppings incorporate various bits of fish for flavoring, and Italians don't mind using canned tuna at all. I've tried several variations of this dish in different places, and find that it tastes better lightly chilled. It's got enough bite to partner good dry rosé as well as a fairly substantial white.

⊰ wine recommendation: grenache rosé, semillon ⊱

15 OUNCES CANNED CANNELLINI BEANS, DRAINED

8-OUNCE CAN WATER-PACKED TUNA, DRAINED

2 TABLESPOONS EXTRA-VIRGIN OLIVE OIL

1/2 CUP ONION, FINELY CHOPPED

1 TEASPOON MINCED FRESH ROSEMARY

1 TABLESPOON FRESH LEMON JUICE

SALT AND FRESHLY GROUND PEPPER TO TASTE

1 BAY LEAF

1 CLOVE GARLIC

~Put the beans in a small bowl. Add the tuna and flake it with a fork. Add the olive oil and mash the ingredients together just enough to break up the beans and integrate the tuna. Stir in the onion, rosemary, lemon juice, salt, and pepper, mixing well. Insert the bay leaf and garlic clove in the mixture. Cover and refrigerate. Remove the bay leaf and garlic before serving.

PROVENÇAL BRUSCHETTA

A strong contender for a universal favorite in Provence is tapenade, the pungent paste made from olives, capers, anchovies, and bits of flavorings. I've toned down the pungency a little here, and if you find anchovies too strong, try soaking them in a little milk for 30 minutes, which takes the funky edge off them. Be sure to use oil-cured olives rather than those canned in brine, which have little flavor. This would go with a more substantial white wine, or even a chilled light red.

◦{ wine recommendation: sauvignon blanc, gigondas }◦

36 BLACK OLIVES, PITTED

3 TABLESPOONS CAPERS, RINSED

6 ANCHOVY FILLETS

½ TEASPOON DRIED THYME

¼ TEASPOON GROUND PEPPER

2 TABLESPOONS FRESH LEMON JUICE

4 TABLESPOONS EXTRA-VIRGIN OLIVE OIL

1 RED BELL PEPPER, SEEDED, ROASTED, PEELED, AND COARSELY CHOPPED (see note, facing page)

~In a blender or food processor, combine the olives, capers, anchovies, thyme, and ground pepper. Process them lightly, pulsing on and off to make a coarse mixture. (You can also chop the ingredients together by hand.) Add the lemon juice and 2 tablespoons of the olive oil. Process again briefly, then add the remaining 2 tablespoons oil and process again briefly, to make a coarse mixture, not a puree. Transfer to a bowl and stir in the red bell pepper.

SPICY AVOCADO-BASIL BRUSCHETTA

Well, why not? The contrast of cool, creamy avocado and warm, crisp bread is a great beginning, and the flavors follow through with a kick. This is best with a higher-acid, somewhat full-bodied white wine.

◦{ wine recommendation: sauvignon blanc }◦

4 AVOCADOS, PEELED AND PITTED

3 TABLESPOONS FRESH LEMON JUICE

4 GREEN ONIONS, GREEN PARTS ONLY, FINELY CHOPPED

1 RED THAI CHILI, SEEDED AND MINCED

24 LEAVES OF FRESH BASIL, TORN INTO PIECES

~In a medium bowl, combine the avocados and the lemon juice. Mash with a fork, leaving some chunks. Stir in all the remaining ingredients, mixing thoroughly. Cover with plastic wrap pressed onto the surface to keep the color bright. Refrigerate for at least 1 hour before serving.

PASTAS

Even the simplest pasta is thoroughly wine-friendly, be it tagliatelle tossed with butter and sage or butter and grated cheese—a frequent first course in northern Italy—or the deliciously basic mix of olive oil, herbs, and slices of peeled tomatoes that often begins a meal in the south. Even old-fashioned baked macaroni and cheese from America makes a good companion. My first choice for any pasta with a hearty sauce would usually be a light red; certainly that would be the best choice in Italy, as most Italian whites lack any sort of amplitude: They're just too light for fairly generous food, and they fade even more as you eat, unable to stand their ground. Wines like Soave are a good choice with simple dishes like pasta tossed with fresh vegetables and herbs, and some Asian noodle dishes, hot or cold, that are usually lightly dressed. (In America, it's possible to have a more substantial white from California, Oregon, or Washington, but that might defeat the purpose of an easygoing first course, turning the overture into a concerto.)

For a casual pasta course meant to open a meal, a light, rather dry (in other words, not too fruity) red would generally be the best choice, something like Dolcetto or Valpolicella, or Beaujolais or Chinon, or a Grenache from Australia; a slight chill, say 30 minutes in the fridge, would help its refreshment value. For a main-course pasta, there are several more options, depending mostly on the sauces; again, most of the time, reds would work best. Pasta salads offer the widest choice: either light-to-medium whites, dry rosés, or light, chillable reds, depending on the salad dressing, your preference, and the occasion.

MUSHROOM, PESTO, AND HAZELNUT LASAGNE

One of the best Italian restaurants in the Pacific Northwest is Nick's Italian Cafe in McMinnville, in the heart of Oregon's wine country. It's down-home, old-fashioned, and slightly funky. This lasagne, simply fabulous, was served at the International Pinot Noir Festival some years back, and after much pleading I got the recipe from chef-owner Nick Peirano. Although it has a lot of ingredients, it's quite easy, really just a matter of making an assemblage. I use dried lasagne, and usually half-and-half wild (chanterelles) and white button mushrooms. It's perfect with a full-flavored light red that would act as a foil to its richness; a heavier-bodied wine wouldn't work nearly as well.

◦{wine recommendation: pinot noir }◦

Serves six
as a
main course

1 CUP PESTO SAUCE (see page 69)

½ CUP RICOTTA CHEESE

BÉCHAMEL SAUCE:

4 CUPS MILK

½ CUP (1 stick) UNSALTED BUTTER

½ CUP ALL-PURPOSE FLOUR

SALT AND FRESHLY GROUND PEPPER TO TASTE

12 OUNCES DRIED LASAGNE NOODLES

1 CUP (4 ounces) GRATED PARMESAN CHEESE

1 CUP (4 OUNCES) FRESHLY GRATED PECORINO ROMANO CHEESE

8 OUNCES MUSHROOMS, CUT INTO ¼-INCH-THICK SLICES

2½ CUPS (12 OUNCES) HAZELNUTS, TOASTED, SKINNED, AND COARSELY CHOPPED (see note)

~Preheat the oven to 400°F. Butter a 9-by-13-inch baking dish.

~In a small bowl, combine the pesto sauce and the ricotta cheese. Mix well. Set aside.

~To make the béchamel: In a small saucepan, heat the milk over medium-low heat until bubbles form around the edges of the pan. In another medium saucepan, melt the butter over medium heat. Gradually whisk in the flour and continue whisking for about 3 minutes or until the mixture turns a golden color. Gradually whisk the hot milk into the mixture until smooth. Continue to whisk until the mixture thickens. Add salt and pepper. Cover and remove from heat.

~In a large pot of boiling salted water, cook the pasta for about 8 minutes, or until al dente. Drain. Meanwhile, mix the 2

cheeses together well. Put a layer of lasagne in the dish, then spread the pesto mixture on top. Add another layer of lasagne and top with the mushrooms. Ladle a thin layer of béchamel over the mushrooms, then sprinkle half of the mixed cheeses over the sauce. Put another layer of lasagne on top and ladle on more béchamel sauce, spreading it to completely cover the pasta (you don't have to use up all the sauce). Sprinkle the top with the remaining cheese and the hazelnuts. Bake for 20 minutes, or until the cheese has melted and browned slightly. Remove from the oven and let sit for 5 to 10 minutes before cutting into squares to serve.

Note: Toasting and skinning hazelnuts: Preheat the oven to 350°F. Spread the hazelnuts in a rimmed baking sheet. Toast in the oven until fragrant, about 8 minutes. Wrap in a clean kitchen towel and rub with the towel to remove most of the skins.

PENNE WITH FONTINA AND PORTOBELLO MUSHROOMS

Italians love baked pasta and cheese as much as we do, but they don't believe in oversimplifying it. This rich concoction is more of a supper than lunch dish. Try it with a side dish of sautéed spinach, matched with a hearty red wine.

⊷{wine recommendation: zinfandel, barbera, barolo, barbaresco}⊷

Serves four

as a

main course

4 TABLESPOONS UNSALTED BUTTER

1 CLOVE GARLIC, MINCED

1 POUND PORTOBELLO MUSHROOMS, THINLY SLICED

10 OUNCES PENNE PASTA

1 TABLESPOON OLIVE OIL

2½ CUPS (10 ounces) SHREDDED ITALIAN FONTINA CHEESE

SALT AND FRESHLY GROUND PEPPER TO TASTE

1 CUP HEAVY CREAM

~In a large sauté pan or skillet, melt the butter over medium heat and sauté the garlic for 1 minute. Add the mushrooms and sauté for about 5 minutes, or until tender. Set aside.

~Preheat the oven to 400°F. Butter an 8-cup baking dish.

~In a large pot of salted boiling water, cook pasta for about 10 minutes, or until al dente. Drain thoroughly. In a medium bowl, toss the pasta with the olive oil. Cover the bottom of the pre-pared baking dish with about one-fourth of the pasta. Scatter one-fourth of the mushrooms over, then one-fourth of the cheese. Sprinkle with salt and pepper. Repeat the layering 3 times, finishing with cheese. Pour the cream over the top. Cover tightly with a sheet of aluminum foil and bake for 15 minutes. Remove the foil and bake for 10 minutes, or until lightly browned. Remove from the oven and let rest for 5 to 10 minutes before serving.

A LIGURIAN TRIO OF PASTA SAUCES

Sestre Levante, the small seaside town in Italy where my wife and I go for a vacation every year, has a tiny shop that turns out an amazing variety of pasta made fresh every day in a little back room just visible through a beaded curtain; there are usually a dozen kinds of round and flat noodles, bow ties, and oddly curled twists, some of them colored from additions to the dough: pink from beet, green from spinach, black from squid ink, and one that's speckled, which is made with pepper. There are always half a dozen sauces too, and the woman behind the counter is quite dogmatic about which sauce goes with which pasta. Over time, I managed to get the secret of three of her best sauces. They go well with a variety of plain pastas.

Note: Each recipe makes enough for 1 pound of dried pasta, which will serve 4 as a main course.

SIMMERED MEAT AND VEGETABLE SAUCE (*TOCCO*)

Tocco means "chunk" or "hunk" in much of Italy, but in Liguria and the coastal part of Tuscany, it means *sauce,* and it rarely involves tomatoes. The beef sauce is actually quite light, though it's got plenty of flavor and aroma. It would make a good first course, served in small bowls with hollow pasta like small macaroni or bucatini (it's quite a liquid sauce, and the pasta should be well drenched), or with more substantial pasta, such as penne or fusilli, as the main course at lunch. As the beef isn't browned, it turns out light and subtle, a very good match for aromatic white wine.

•{ wine recommendation: pinot grigio, vermentino }•

½ OUNCE DRIED PORCINI MUSHROOMS

1 CUP BOILING WATER

1 TABLESPOON OLIVE OIL

1 SMALL ONION, CHOPPED

1 CARROT, CHOPPED

1 STALK CELERY, CHOPPED

1 LARGE CLOVE GARLIC, MINCED

2 TABLESPOONS MINCED FRESH PARSLEY

8 OUNCES LEAN GROUND BEEF

1 TEASPOON MINCED FRESH THYME

½ CUP DRY WHITE WINE

1 TABLESPOON FLOUR

SALT AND FRESHLY GROUND PEPPER TO TASTE

1 CUP CANNED LOW-SALT BEEF BROTH

~Put the mushrooms in a bowl, pour the boiling water over them, and let them soak for about 30 minutes. Meanwhile, heat the olive oil in a medium, heavy saucepan over low heat. Add the onion, carrot, and celery. Cover and cook for about 20 minutes. Add the garlic and parsley and cook, uncovered, for 5 minutes, mixing well. Add the ground beef, breaking it up well with a wooden spoon. Sprinkle in the thyme and mix well. Add the wine, increase heat to medium, and cook, stirring occasionally, until the wine has nearly evaporated.

~Meanwhile, remove the reconstituted mushrooms from the water, squeeze dry over the bowl, and chop coarsely. Add the mushrooms and 3 tablespoons of the soaking water to the meat. Sprinkle the flour over, add salt and pepper, mix well, and add just enough beef broth to cover. Reduce heat to low and simmer for 30 minutes, stirring from time to time (the sauce will develop a skin occasionally; just stir it back into the sauce, which enriches it). When done, the sauce will still be quite liquid; serve it over pasta in warmed shallow bowls, without adding cheese.

CREAMY WALNUT SAUCE

This is the sauce I like best for a summer Sunday three-course lunch of stuffed pasta, such as spinach, chard, or even pumpkin ravioli; sliced tomatoes and mozzarella cheese sprinkled with olive oil, chopped fresh basil, and a squeeze of lemon; and slices of zucchini sautéed with garlic and pine nuts—a nice mix of flavors, with chunks of bread to mop up the various juices. The usual base for this recipe is a local soft, tangy cheese that isn't exported; the substitution used elsewhere in Italy is curdled milk (which you can make by adding a squeeze of lemon to warm milk), but it seems too bland compared with the original. My solution, after a lot of experimenting, is buttermilk, which has the perfect tangy bite. Most days, we drink light, aromatic white wines with this one, though a cooled light red would match up well too.

{ wine recommendation: pinot grigio, valpolicella }

1 CUP (4 ounces) WALNUT HALVES

1 SLICE WHITE BREAD, CRUST REMOVED

1/2 TEASPOON SALT

1 TEASPOON MINCED FRESH MARJORAM

1/4 CUP EXTRA-VIRGIN OLIVE OIL

1/2 CUP BUTTERMILK

~Put the walnuts in a blender or food processor. Moisten the bread well with water, tear it into pieces, and add to the nuts. Process briefly. Add the salt, marjoram, olive oil, and buttermilk, and process well to make a creamy sauce.

HEARTY PESTO SAUCE

Pesto sauce originated in Liguria, where an incredible profusion of herbs perfumes the hillside air; in the open-air markets of the towns, enormous bunches of basil sell for less than a dollar, and the locals put it in everything—I've even had basil ice cream, which is odd but delicious. These days, versions of the sauce in America and other parts of Italy tend to be rich and heavy on the cheese, but this is the way they still make it in Sestre Levante. A nice touch is to toast 1 tablespoon of pine nuts in a pie pan for 4 or 5 minutes in a preheated 350°F oven, then sprinkle them over the finished dish as a garnish.

Basil has an affinity with smooth and savory medium-strength red wines.

{ wine recommendation: rosso de montalcino, dolcetto, barbera d'alba, valpolicella, california sangiovese, oregon or california pinot noir }

1 CUP TIGHTLY PACKED FRESH BASIL LEAVES

1 LARGE CLOVE GARLIC, COARSELY CHOPPED

2 TABLESPOONS PINE NUTS

1/2 CUP EXTRA-VIRGIN OLIVE OIL

2 TABLESPOONS FRESHLY GRATED PARMESAN CHEESE

SALT TO TASTE

~In a food processor, combine the basil leaves, garlic, and pine nuts, and pulse on and off to chop and mix the ingredients. Add 1/4 cup of the oil, process for 1 minute, and then add the remaining 1/4 cup oil and the cheese and process thoroughly to make a smooth sauce. Taste for salt (a pinch or two may bring out the flavor of the cheese). The sauce should be more of a liquid than a puree; if you need to add more olive oil, put the sauce into a bowl and whisk the oil in by hand, 1 tablespoon at a time.

FUSILLI SALADE NIÇOISE

Elizabeth David once wrote, with some asperity, that there was no recipe for salade niçoise: Cooks simply used what was on hand, and as anyone who's ever visited a southern French town on market day knows, that's a complicated bounty. Across the border, along the sunny coast of Italy, this dish is sometimes even more free-form, as I discovered one day in an open-air beachfront café, where I had this wonderful mixture made with pasta rather than the usual potatoes. It's a first-rate partner for a refreshing rosé.

⋅{wine recommendation: bandol, california zinfandel, australian grenache rosé}⋅

Serves four
as a
main course

1 TEASPOON DIJON MUSTARD

1 TABLESPOON RED WINE VINEGAR

3 TABLESPOONS OLIVE OIL

1 EIGHT-OUNCE TUNA FILLET

1 POUND FUSILLI PASTA

8 ANCHOVY FILLETS, DRAINED AND COARSELY CHOPPED

½ RED ONION, SLICED THINLY

1 RED BELL PEPPER, SEEDED, DERIBBED, AND COARSELY CHOPPED

2 STALKS CELERY, CHOPPED

3 ROMA (plum) TOMATOES, QUARTERED AND SEEDED

18 NIÇOISE OLIVES, PITTED AND HALVED

DRESSING:

6 TABLESPOONS EXTRA-VIRGIN OLIVE OIL

2 TABLESPOONS FRESH LEMON JUICE

12 LEAVES FRESH BASIL, CHOPPED

1 CLOVE GARLIC, MINCED

GENEROUS PINCH OF SUGAR OR TO TASTE

SALT AND FRESHLY GROUND PEPPER TO TASTE

2 HARD-COOKED EGGS, QUARTERED

~In a small bowl, mix the first 3 ingredients together. Rub the tuna with the marinade and let sit at room temperature for 1 hour.

~Preheat the broiler. Broil the tuna 4 inches from the heat source for 3 minutes on each side, or until browned on the outside but medium rare on the inside. Transfer to a bowl and break the tuna into chunks with a fork. (If fresh tuna is unavailable, use canned albacore tuna, drain, break it up, marinate the chunks for 1 hour, and drain again.)

~In a large pot of salted boiling water, cook the pasta for about 10 minutes, or until al dente. Drain, rinse with cold water, drain again, and put in a large bowl. Toss with a little oil to coat. Add the tuna, anchovies, and vegetables.

~To make the dressing, whisk the oil, lemon juice, basil, and garlic together. Season with sugar, salt, and pepper. Pour over the salad and toss thoroughly. Cover (the basil fragrance will permeate the salad) and refrigerate for at least 1 hour or up to 2 hours. Garnish with the eggs to serve.

SWEET PEPPER AND SAUSAGE PASTA SALAD

When summer comes, I cook on the barbecue most of the time, and rather than waste the heat of the coals, I tend to grill vegetables for future use. Marinated grilled peppers are the sweet flavoring in this colorful salad, which tastes best at room temperature or slightly chilled, just like the ideal wine match, which is light, soft, and very fruity.

⟨ wine recommendation: beaujolais ⟩

8 OUNCES SWEET (not hot) ITALIAN SAUSAGE

1 POUND MACARONI OR ROTELLE PASTA

1 FENNEL BULB, TRIMMED

MARINATED BELL PEPPERS, DRAINED (recipe follows)

1/2 CUP CHOPPED GREEN ONIONS, INCLUDING LIGHT GREEN PARTS

DRESSING:

6 TABLESPOONS EXTRA-VIRGIN OLIVE OIL

2 TABLESPOONS FRESH LEMON JUICE

1 TABLESPOON CHOPPED FRESH THYME

6 PIECES OIL-PACKED SUN-DRIED TOMATOES, DRAINED AND COARSELY CHOPPED

1 CLOVE GARLIC, MINCED

GENEROUS PINCH OF SUGAR, OR TO TASTE

1/4 CUP PINE NUTS, TOASTED (see note)

Serves four as a main course

~Light a fire in a charcoal grill or preheat the broiler. Grill or broil the sausages until well browned on all sides. Cut into 1-inch pieces. Set aside.

~In a large pot of salted boiling water, cook the pasta for about 10 minutes, or until al dente. Drain, rinse with cold water, and drain again.

~Meanwhile, in a small bowl, whisk the dressing ingredients together.

~Cut into the fennel bulb lengthwise most of the way down to the base at 1/4-inch intervals, then across the same way. Turn the bulb on its side and cut across at 1-inch intervals to make matchstick-shaped pieces; discard the base. In a large bowl, combine the pasta, sausage, peppers, fennel, green onions, and dressing. Toss well. Divide the salad among 4 plates and sprinkle each with pine nuts.

MARINATED BELL PEPPERS:

2 RED BELL PEPPERS, HALVED, SEEDED, AND DERIBBED

2 YELLOW BELL PEPPERS, HALVED, SEEDED, AND DERIBBED

ABOUT 1/2 CUP OLIVE OIL

1 TABLESPOON ALLSPICE BERRIES

GRATED ZEST AND JUICE OF 1 LEMON

4 BAY LEAVES

4 CLOVES GARLIC

~Light a fire in a charcoal grill or preheat the broiler. Place the peppers on the grill or on a broiler pan lined with aluminum foil. Grill or broil, turning as necessary until evenly charred. Transfer to a plastic bag to cool for 15 minutes. Peel and cut the peppers in strips about 2 inches long and 1/2 inch wide.

~Pour about 1/4 cup of the olive oil into a 1-quart jar. Add half of the allspice, half of the lemon zest, 1 of the bay leaves, and 1 clove of garlic. Layer the remaining peppers, allspice, zest, bay leaves, and garlic on top. Pour in the lemon juice and the remaining olive oil until the mixture is just covered. To serve, drain and discard liquid and flavorings. Cover and refrigerate for at least 3 days or up to 1 week.

Note: Toasting pine nuts: Preheat the oven to 350°F. Spread the nuts on a pie pan and toast in the oven for 4 or 5 minutes.

RICE

Despite its popularity, not everyone has been in favor of rice. The irritable philosopher Friedrich Nietzsche declared that eating it led to opium smoking, while the great gourmet Brillat-Savarin insisted that rice "saps the moral fiber and even courage" (but then, the French have never understood rice). No amount of research has turned up similar irrational musings from an Italian.

Rice is the staple food of more than half the world. It's grown in dozens of countries with wildly different cuisines and is the bedrock many of them rest on. How then, after about five thousand years of wide-open culinary opportunities, was it the Italians—fairly late entrants into the game, it should be noted—who elevated it to glory by inventing risotto? The only possible answer is genius: Risotto seems to have been invented during the Renaissance, when brilliance was fairly common currency.

Rice becomes risotto because of the starch in several varieties of medium-grain rice, which dissolves during cooking and creates a creamy, clinging texture as the grains of rice absorb the liquid. Some varieties soak up as much as twice their weight, which makes it vital that first-rate stock and good wine are used. Arborio rice is widely known, and good for thoroughly creamy risottos because of its high percentage of starch; Vialone Nano has less starch and makes a looser, drier risotto, but absorbs the most water (and therefore flavor) and thus needs little stirring; Carnaroli is highly prized for its slightly finer texture, but is not exactly traditional: it's a cross of Vialone and a Japanese strain, developed in 1945 by a Milanese. Whichever one is used, remember that the consistency of risotto is a matter of personal choice: Some like it to have a fairly firm and stodgy texture, others like it more liquid and creamy. It's up to you. The following risottos are meant to be served as main dishes. Some vegetarian risottos are found in the next section, on the theory that those are more likely to be used as side dishes with meats or fish.

Some dishes made with long-grain white rice also work nicely with wine, notably the spicy Cajun jambalaya and Spanish paella (in both those cases, the spiciness and mixture of flavors dictate a fairly substantial, four-square sort of wine, like Sauvignon Blanc). Kedgeree, the strongly flavored Anglo-Indian dish, is also a good match, as well as being a nice offbeat choice for part of a buffet or lunch; an elegant version is included in this chapter.

TIGER PRAWNS AND CELERY RISOTTO

This is a fresh-tasting and fairly light risotto. Seafood risottos should be a bit more liquid than meat or vegetable ones, so it may be necessary to add a bit more broth or water at the end. Cheese is never added to seafood risotto. The prawns are added at the end to keep them from overcooking, but using the shells in the broth ensures that the flavor comes through. Given the assertiveness of the prawns and celery, a tart white makes a good partner.

{wine recommendation: sauvignon blanc }

Serves four
as a
main course

8 OUNCES TIGER PRAWNS

1 CUP WATER

6 CUPS CANNED LOW-SALT CHICKEN BROTH

1 TABLESPOON UNSALTED BUTTER

2 TABLESPOONS OLIVE OIL

1 ONION, FINELY CHOPPED

2 STALKS CELERY, CHOPPED

2 CUPS ARBORIO RICE

1 CUP DRY WHITE WINE

1 TABLESPOON MINCED FRESH CHIVES

1 TABLESPOON MINCED FRESH PARSLEY

~Shell and devein the prawns, reserving the shells. In a small saucepan, combine the reserved shells and the water. Bring to a simmer and cook for 5 minutes; they'll turn pink. Strain the liquid and discard the shells. Add the chicken broth. Bring to a simmer on a back burner.

~In a medium, heavy saucepan, melt the butter with the olive oil over low heat. Add the onion and cook for about 5 minutes, or until soft. Add the celery and rice to the pan, stir vigorously, and cook, stirring, until opaque, 2 or 3 minutes. Add the wine and cook, stirring constantly, until it is almost evaporated. Begin adding 1/2 cup of the broth at a time, cooking each addition until almost all the liquid is absorbed, and stirring frequently to keep it from sticking. After about 20 minutes, test the rice for doneness; it should be tender but firm to the bite. If it's not done, stir in another 1/2 cup liquid—use water if all the broth has been used—and cook another few minutes. Cut the prawns in half crosswise and add to the pan, stirring well. Cook for a further 2 minutes, or until the prawns are pink. Remove from heat and stir in the chives. Serve in warmed shallow bowls, garnished with a sprinkling of parsley.

VERONESE SAUSAGE RISOTTO

There are still plenty of wild boars up in the mountains of northern Italy, and they love grapes, so the hunting season coincides with the autumn harvest. In the spring, the locals evaluate the quality of the wild-boar sausage by cooking it into a risotto like this one, which I was served in Verona. It's relatively light, so the best match would be a similar red.

{wine recommendation: valpolicella superioré}

7 CUPS CANNED LOW-SALT CHICKEN BROTH

1 TABLESPOON UNSALTED BUTTER

2 TABLESPOONS OLIVE OIL

1 ONION, FINELY CHOPPED

2 CUPS ARBORIO RICE

8 OUNCES SWEET (not hot) ITALIAN SAUSAGE, REMOVED FROM CASING

4 OUNCES MUSHROOMS, SLICED

1 CUP DRY WHITE WINE

1 TABLESPOON MINCED FRESH SAGE

3 TABLESPOONS FRESHLY GRATED PARMESAN CHEESE

2 TABLESPOONS CHOPPED FRESH PARSLEY

Serves four as a main course

~In a small saucepan, bring the chicken broth to a simmer on a back burner and maintain the simmer over low heat. In a medium, heavy saucepan, melt the butter with the olive oil over low heat. Add the onion and cook until soft, about 5 minutes. Increase heat to medium and add the rice and sausage meat to the pan, stirring them in vigorously. Cook, stirring, until the rice is opaque, 2 or 3 minutes. Add the mushrooms, stir in the wine, and continue stirring until the wine is almost evaporated. Begin adding $1/2$ cup of the broth at a time, cooking each addition until almost all the liquid is absorbed and stirring frequently to keep the rice from sticking.

~After about 20 minutes, stir in the sage. Taste the rice for doneness; the rice should be tender but firm to the bite. If it's not done, stir in another $1/2$ cup liquid—use water if all the broth has been used—and cook another few minutes. Remove the pan from heat and stir in the cheese. Serve in warmed shallow bowls, garnished with a sprinkling of parsley.

PIQUANT ARUGULA AND PECORINO RISOTTO

Umbria is the region just southeast of Tuscany, landlocked, mountainous, and dotted with lovely small towns known more for Renaissance art than for gastronomy, like Spoleto and Assisi. The famous wine town is Orvieto, but the best Umbrian wine is made near the ancient town of Torgiano by the Lungarotti family, which also operates a fascinating wine museum and an elegant restaurant, Le Tre Vaselle, where I got this recipe for a unique risotto.

Pecorino Romano is a tangy sheep's-milk cheese, and combining it with arugula, which has a slightly peppery bite, is a brilliant idea. It's a good dish on its own, but I also like to serve this risotto alongside lamb chops marinated in olive oil, rosemary, and garlic, and broiled. The ideal partner is an assertive red, but with some finesse to it.

{wine recommendation: rubesco, from lungarotti, or california or washington syrah }

Serves four
as a
main course,
six as a side dish

7 CUPS CANNED LOW-SALT BEEF BROTH

4 TABLESPOONS UNSALTED BUTTER

2 TABLESPOONS FINELY CHOPPED ONION

2 CUPS ARBORIO RICE

1 CUP DRY WHITE WINE

4 OUNCES ARUGULA, COARSELY CHOPPED

8 OUNCES FRESHLY GRATED PECORINO ROMANO CHEESE

SALT AND FRESHLY GROUND PEPPER TO TASTE

~In a medium saucepan, bring the broth to a simmer on a back burner. In a medium, heavy saucepan, melt 3 tablespoons of the butter over medium heat. Add the onion and sauté until soft, about 3 minutes. Add the rice and cook, stirring, until opaque, 2 to 3 minutes. Add the white wine and cook, stirring, until the wine has almost evaporated. Begin adding the broth, $1/2$ cup at a time, cooking each addition until almost all the liquid is absorbed, and stirring frequently to keep the rice from sticking. After about 20 minutes, test the rice for doneness; it should be tender but firm to the bite. If not, stir in another $1/2$ cup liquid—use water if all the broth has been used—and cook for another 1 or 2 minutes. Add the arugula, the remaining 1 tablespoon butter, and cheese. Stir well and season with salt and pepper. Serve in warmed shallow bowls as a main course, or alongside other food as a side dish.

SALMON AND PRAWN KEDGEREE

This dish got its name from an Indian word for "mish-mash," and its subsequent history is one of living up to the name. The British aristocracy made it a breakfast staple in Victorian times. It was also popular in the Netherlands and Denmark, two countries that like abundant buffets and spicy food. It's usually served warm but works quite well at room temperature, so it's a blessing for parties, or as part of a Sunday brunch or a casual supper. Partner it best with a fruity, lively, and aromatic white wine.

wine recommendation: gerwürztraminer, german riesling, champagne

Serves four
as a
light main course

2 TABLESPOONS UNSALTED BUTTER

1 ONION, CHOPPED

1 TEASPOON CURRY POWDER

1 CUP BASMATI RICE

2 CUPS BOILING WATER

½ CUP HEAVY CREAM OR HALF-AND-HALF

8 OUNCES SMOKED SALMON, CUT INTO ½-INCH PIECES

8 OUNCES JUMBO SHRIMP, COOKED, SHELLED, AND HALVED CROSSWISE

3 HARD-COOKED EGGS, FINELY CHOPPED

1 TABLESPOON MINCED FRESH PARSLEY

3 TABLESPOONS MINCED FRESH CHIVES

~In a medium saucepan, melt the butter over medium heat. Add the onion and sauté until soft, about 5 minutes. Sprinkle the curry powder over and mix thoroughly. Stir in the rice and water. Cover, reduce heat to low, and cook for 11 minutes. Remove from heat and let sit, covered, for 5 minutes.

~Stir the cream or half-and-half into the rice. Gently fold in the salmon, shrimp, and eggs. Smoothly mound onto a serving platter. If serving immediately, sprinkle with parsley and chives, or let it cool, cover, and refrigerate for up to 1 hour. Remove from refrigerator at least 10 minutes before serving, and garnish.

VEGETABLES

Vegetarian dishes are often overlooked by wine experts, which is a bit silly—the same principles of judging and matching flavor, balance, texture, and complexity apply, and the results can be terrific. Mainly, the wines you choose should be relatively light and not too acidic, since most vegetarian meals are low in fats and oils and are subtly flavored. At my house, we diet by cooking vegetarian meals a couple of times a week, and we don't forego wine, either—at about 125 calories for a generous glass of wine, it's easy enough to have a proper meal.

Some vegetables have more of an affinity to wine than others, as noted in the "What Wine?" section earlier, and the way they're cooked can also be a factor, so it's important to keep that in mind: Slow cooking can modify the slightly sulfurous flavors of onions, shallots, and garlic, for example, turning them sweet and very wine-friendly (the difference between onions fried for 5 minutes at high heat or simmered in a little olive oil for 20 minutes is that you'll never fry them again once you taste them simmered).

Mushrooms can taste a little too earthy when raw, but are voluptuous and amiable when cooked. Carrots and most other root vegetables lose their slightly bitter edge and become sweeter, too (this can be helped along with the addition of a little sugar, or even a spoonful of honey or maple syrup during cooking, for extra flavor). When these are added to the less-friendly vegetables, easier matches are made: Slow-cooked carrots, parsnips, and onions, for example, act as modifiers when tossed with cabbage or broccoli, and make those greens better companions to wine.

The best idea when composing a menu is to look at the whole plate. Too many times, in my experience, people simply choose a wine according to the main ingredient—the meat or fish or bird—and let it go at that. Some vegetables, especially the range of bitter greens like broccoli and green cabbage and bok choy, can flatten wine or even make it taste a bit unpleasant, and some assertive Asian spices can make red wine taste downright weird. Basically, the more complex the wine, the more simple the supporting flavors should be; a vegetable stir-fried in a little good olive oil and tossed with herbs, or steamed and tossed with butter and herbs, is really more elegant than an elaborate preparation, because it helps show off the interplay of the main dish and the wine, like a first-rate chorus behind a pair of great singers.

ALMOND-PARMESAN STUFFED ONIONS

In Italy, this would be a separate course in a banquet or large meal, but I've found it also makes a good first course with the addition of a little pasta—it's especially good in winter, when its savory and sweet flavors get a robust meal off to a hearty start. The wine of choice for me here is a fresh, lively red that can match the flavors step for step.

{wine recommendation: pinot noir }

Serves six
as a
first course

6 LARGE ONIONS

1 ½ CUPS FRESH BREAD CRUMBS, SOAKED IN ½ CUP MILK

3 LARGE EGGS, LIGHTLY BEATEN

¾ CUP (3 ounces) FRESHLY GRATED PARMESAN CHEESE

¼ CUP FINELY GROUND ALMONDS

LARGE PINCH OF GROUND CLOVES

LARGE PINCH OF SUGAR

1 LARGE EGG YOLK BEATEN WITH 2 TABLESPOONS MILK

6 TEASPOONS UNSALTED BUTTER

½ CUP SMALL PASTA, SUCH AS FARFALLINE OR ORZO, OR ANGEL-HAIR PASTA BROKEN INTO 1-INCH LENGTHS

~Preheat the oven to 400°F. Trim the top of the onions, but leave the root end intact. Peel the onions. In a large saucepan of boiling water to cover, cook the onions for 5 minutes. Remove from the water, let cool, and cut 1 inch off the top of each. Scoop out the interior, leaving a thin shell. Finely chop the tops and interiors. In a medium bowl, combine the chopped onion, soaked bread crumbs, eggs, cheese, almonds, cloves, and sugar. Stir thoroughly. Stuff the cavity of each onion with the filling, packing it down.

~Place the onions in a buttered baking dish. Brush the outside of each onion with the egg mixture and top with 1 teaspoon of the butter. Cover loosely with aluminum foil and bake for 1 ½ hours. Just before the onions are done, cook the pasta in a medium pot of salted boiling water for about 10 minutes, or until al dente. Drain. To serve, transfer the onions to individual bowls, toss the cooked pasta in the pan juices, and spoon some pasta around the base of each onion.

FARMERS' MARKET PASTA

This is one of the best hearty vegetarian pasta dishes I've ever had. It's from La Cantinetta Antinori restaurant in Florence, where the Antinori family has been making wine since 1385. It's slightly chunky and has some heft to it, but the flavors are fairly sophisticated, and the wines that match the profile of this dish are red, medium bodied, and definitely Tuscan.

{wine recommendation: chianti, rosso di montalcino }

Serves six

as a

main course

2 TABLESPOONS UNSALTED BUTTER

2 TABLESPOONS OLIVE OIL

1 ONION, FINELY CHOPPED

1 CLOVE GARLIC, MINCED

1 GLOBE EGGPLANT, CUT INTO ½-INCH DICE

3 RED BELL PEPPERS, SEEDED, DERIBBED, AND FINELY CHOPPED

2 CARROTS, FINELY DICED

2 ZUCCHINI, THINLY SLICED

1 CUP FRESH BASIL LEAVES, CHOPPED

LEAVES FROM 1 SPRIG THYME

1 CUP DRY WHITE WINE

3 TABLESPOONS TOMATO PASTE

SALT AND FRESHLY GROUND PEPPER TO TASTE

1 POUND TUBE PASTA, SUCH AS PENNE, MACARONI, OR FUSILLI

½ CUP FRESHLY GRATED PARMESAN CHEESE

~In a large skillet, melt the butter with the oil over medium heat. Add the onion and sauté for about 6 minutes, or until soft and beginning to brown. Add the garlic and sauté for 2 or 3 minutes more. Add the eggplant, bell peppers, carrots, and zucchini and cook, stirring often, for about 10 minutes, or until the vegetables are almost tender. Stir in the basil and thyme, then the wine, tomato paste, salt, and pepper. Reduce heat to low and simmer for 10 minutes.

~Meanwhile, in a large pot of salted boiling water, cook the pasta for about 10 minutes, or until al dente. Drain. Transfer to a bowl. Add the vegetables and mix lightly, sprinkling with half of the Parmesan. Serve the remaining cheese at table.

GAZPACHO

This Spanish specialty is one of the few soups that goes with wine, not only because of its interplay of flavors, but also its chunky texture, more like real food than most soups. It comes from Andalusia, in the same southern part of the country that gave us flamenco dancing and sherry—which is its natural partner. This soup and a chilled, bone-dry sherry are the perfect way to start a summer supper.

⟨ wine recommendation: fino, manzanilla ⟩

3 SLICES DAY-OLD SOURDOUGH BREAD, CRUSTS TRIMMED

2 POUNDS TOMATOES, PEELED, SEEDED, AND CHOPPED

3 TABLESPOONS SHERRY VINEGAR

3 GREEN BELL PEPPERS, SEEDED, DERIBBED, AND CHOPPED

1 CUCUMBER, PEELED, SEEDED, AND CHOPPED

3 TABLESPOONS EXTRA-VIRGIN OLIVE OIL

2 CUPS WATER

1 CUP TOMATO JUICE

1 RED ONION, CHOPPED

1 CUP SLICED ALMONDS, TOASTED (see Note)

Serves six as a first course

~Tear the bread into pieces. In a blender or food processor, combine the bread, tomatoes, vinegar, two-thirds of the bell peppers, two-thirds of the cucumber, the olive oil, and water. Puree the mixture until smooth.

~Pour the puree into a medium bowl. Add the tomato juice and stir well. Cover and refrigerate for at least 2 hours. Place the remaining cucumber, peppers, and the onion in separate bowls. Cover and refrigerate along with the gazpacho. Just before serving, stir in the almonds. Pour the soup into individual bowls. Pass the bowls of vegetables around for each person to garnish individually.

Note: Toasting sliced almonds: Preheat the oven to 350°F. Spread the nuts in a rimmed baking sheet and toast in the oven, stirring once or twice, until lightly toasted, 4 to 5 minutes.

RED PEPPER FLAN

Northern Italians love to play around with savory custards, combinations of eggs, spices, cheese, and whatever vegetables take their fancy. In northwestern Italy, where they have intensely sweet red peppers, this is a favorite. It makes a terrific and offbeat first course, garnished with a wreath of mixed greens. A light but aromatic white wine is a very good match.

∘{ wine recommendation: viognier }∘

3 LARGE RED BELL PEPPERS, HALVED, SEEDED, AND DERIBBED

2 TABLESPOONS UNSALTED BUTTER

2 TABLESPOONS FLOUR

⅔ CUP MILK

3 LARGE EGGS, LIGHTLY BEATEN

6 TABLESPOONS FRESHLY GRATED PARMESAN CHEESE

¼ TEASPOON SALT

¼ TEASPOON FRESHLY GROUND PEPPER

¼ TEASPOON FRESHLY GROUND NUTMEG

2 HANDFULS MIXED SALAD GREENS FOR GARNISH

1 TABLESPOON EXTRA-VIRGIN OLIVE OIL

Serves six as a main course

~Preheat the oven to 375°F. Place the peppers on a baking sheet and bake for 45 minutes. Let cool and peel. Place on a triple thickness of paper towels for 30 minutes to drain, which intensifies the flavor. Puree in a blender or food processor.

~Preheat the oven to 375°F. Generously butter six 4-ounce molds.

~In a medium, heavy saucepan, melt the butter over medium-low heat and whisk in the flour. Stir constantly for 2 to 3 minutes, then gradually whisk in the milk and continue whisking until thickened. Remove from heat. Whisk in the red pepper puree. Whisk in the eggs, then the cheese and seasonings until smooth. (If making it ahead, let cool, cover, and refrigerate for up to 2 hours. Bring to room temperature, lightly whisk, and proceed.)

~Set the molds in a baking pan and pour the mix into the prepared molds nearly up to the rim. Place the pan in the oven and pour boiling water into the pan to come two-thirds of the way up the outside of the molds. Bake, uncovered, for about 30 minutes, or until the custards are puffed up and set. Remove the molds from the pan and let them rest for 1 minute. Unmold by running a knife around the inside of each mold, placing a serving plate on top and inverting the mold and plate. Toss the greens with the olive oil and garnish each plate. Serve immediately.

WARM SALAD OF ZUCCHINI, TOMATO, AND BASIL

Here's an appealing combination of flavors, textures, and temperatures, nicely complex but still lively, too. The cheese is there almost as a condiment, to add a slightly salty accent. This is a good dish for a light and slightly herbal white wine.

{wine recommendation: sauvignon blanc}

2 ZUCCHINI, HALVED LENGTHWISE

2 TABLESPOONS EXTRA-VIRGIN OLIVE OIL

6 GREEN ONIONS, CHOPPED, INCLUDING
PALE GREEN PARTS

1 RED BELL PEPPER, SEEDED, DERIBBED, AND DICED

8 CHERRY TOMATOES, HALVED

LEAVES FROM 1 HEAD RED-LEAF LETTUCE, TORN

12 FRESH LEAVES BASIL, CUT INTO FINE SHREDS

¼ CUP CRUMBLED BLUE CHEESE

2 TABLESPOONS PINE NUTS

GRATED ZEST OF 1 LEMON

FRESHLY GROUND PEPPER TO TASTE

1 TEASPOON FRESH LEMON JUICE

Serves two as a first course

~Cut the zucchini into ¼-inch-thick slices. Heat 1 tablespoon of the olive oil in a skillet over medium heat and sauté the zucchini, green onions, and red bell pepper for 10 minutes, or until soft. Add the tomatoes and toss for 2 or 3 minutes, or until heated through and thoroughly mixed. Remove from heat.

~Make a bed of lettuce leaves on each salad plate and spoon the vegetables on top. Sprinkle the basil leaves over, then the cheese, pine nuts, lemon zest, and pepper. Mix the lemon juice with the remaining 1 tablespoon olive oil and drizzle over the salad.

CHUNKY GRILLED SALAD WITH EGGPLANT SAUCE

A mixture of grilled vegetables makes a good salad, and a dressing of eggplant puree gives it a sweet-and-hot underlay of flavor that ties it all together. The combination of firm textures from broiling or grilling and the flavor of the eggplant base make this dish a good match for a light fruity red wine. The wine will taste even better slightly cooled, after spending 30 minutes in the fridge. A loaf of sourdough bread completes the meal beautifully.

{ wine recommendation: beaujolais }

3 GLOBE EGGPLANTS

2 RED BELL PEPPERS, QUARTERED
LENGTHWISE AND SEEDED

4 ROMA (plum) TOMATOES, QUARTERED

2 ZUCCHINI, EACH CUT INTO 6 DIAGONAL SLICES

¼ CUP PLUS 2 TABLESPOONS OLIVE OIL, PLUS
OLIVE OIL FOR BRUSHING

SALT AND FRESHLY GROUND PEPPER TO TASTE

24 FRESH LEAVES BASIL

1 RED THAI CHILI, MINCED

2 TEASPOONS FRESH LEMON JUICE

Serves two as a light main course

~Light a fire in a charcoal grill or preheat the broiler.

~Cut 1 eggplant into quarters lengthwise, then cut crosswise into ½-inch pieces. Cut the bell pepper quarters into ½-inch crosswise pieces. In a large bowl, combine the eggplant, bell pepper, tomatoes, and zucchini. Add the ¼ cup olive oil, salt, and pepper. Toss to coat. Set aside.

~Cut the remaining 2 eggplants in half lengthwise and brush the cut side with olive oil. Grill until the skin is charred and the flesh softened and cooked, about 20 minutes. Or, place them onto a baking sheet, cut-side down, and broil about 4 inches

from the heat source for about 20 minutes. Let cool and peel off the skin. In a blender or food processor, puree the eggplant with 1 tablespoon of the remaining olive oil, 12 leaves of the basil, the chili, and salt to taste. Stir in 1 teaspoon of the lemon juice to preserve the color.

~Put the vegetables in one layer in a grill basket and cook for about 4 minutes on each side over the coals, or until they're lightly charred. Or, spread the vegetables in one layer on a broiler pan. Broil for about 4 minutes, then turn the vegetables over with a metal spatula and broil for 4 minutes on the second side. Remove from broiler. Mix the remaining 1 tablespoon olive oil and 1 teaspoon lemon juice together, tear the remaining basil leaves into pieces, and sprinkle both over the vegetables.

~Spread the eggplant puree onto plates and arrange the grilled vegetables on top. Serve warm.

GREEN HERB RISOTTO

There's a little café near the ferry depot in Venice that fills up every day just before noon. The regulars know that the cook makes just one pot of superb risotto, from different vegetables, depending on what's good in the market that morning; when the pot's empty, he goes home. For a couple of dollars, it's the best lesson on the art of risotto that I know—and the cheapest pleasure in Venice. Vegetable risottos are a little different from other versions. The flavors of vegetables are subtle, so timing is important (if you throw in all the vegetables too soon, some of the flavor and texture can fade), and the spices and condiments need to be somewhat more assertive, to boost the overall impact. Starchy vegetables can make risotto stodgy, so crunchy green ones are often the best.

This is one of my favorite risottos, light and fresh, with a nice chunky texture. Sauvignon Blanc, with its herbal overtones, is a good partner, especially the lighter versions from California and Chile.

{ wine recommendation: sauvignon blanc }

8 CUPS CANNED LOW-SALT CHICKEN BROTH OR VEGETABLE BROTH (recipe follows)

2 TABLESPOONS EXTRA-VIRGIN OLIVE OIL

1 LEEK, WHITE PART ONLY, CHOPPED

1 TABLESPOON MINCED FRESH PARSLEY

1 TEASPOON MINCED FRESH BASIL OR OREGANO

1 TEASPOON MINCED FRESH ROSEMARY

1 STALK CELERY, CHOPPED

2 CUPS ARBORIO RICE

1 CUP DRY WHITE WINE

1 CUP THAWED FROZEN BABY PEAS

1 HEAD BROCCOLI, CUT INTO FLORETS

2 TABLESPOONS GRATED PARMESAN CHEESE

Serves four as a main course

~In a medium saucepan, bring the broth to a simmer on a back burner. Heat the oil in a medium, heavy pot over medium heat and sauté the leek and herbs for 2 or 3 minutes. Add the celery and rice. Cook, stirring, for 2 or 3 minutes, or until the rice is opaque. Add the wine and cook, stirring constantly, until almost evaporated. Add the peas and stir in $1/2$ cup of the broth. Stir frequently until it is nearly absorbed. Continue adding the broth $1/2$ a cup at a time, stirring frequently until each addition is absorbed.

~After about 20 minutes, steam the broccoli florets for 4 minutes. Test the rice for doneness; it should be firm but tender. If not, add $1/2$ cup liquid—use water if the broth has been used up—and cook 1 or 2 minutes longer. Serve the risotto in warmed shallow soup bowls garnished with the broccoli and with a light sprinkling of cheese on top.

VEGETABLE BROTH FOR RISOTTO

If you're not a strict vegetarian, chicken broth is best
in vegetable risottos; if you are, here is a good
basic vegetable broth.

> 2 LEEKS
>
> 3 STALKS CELERY
>
> 6 CARROTS
>
> 2 ONIONS
>
> 1 FENNEL BULB, OR 2 TABLESPOONS FENNEL SEED
>
> 1 HEAD LETTUCE
>
> 1 BUNCH PARSLEY
>
> 4 SPRIGS THYME
>
> 2 BAY LEAVES
>
> 2½ QUARTS WATER

Makes about eight cups

~Coarsely chop the vegetables and parsley. In a stockpot, combine
all the ingredients and bring the water to a boil. Partially cover
the pot, reduce heat to a low simmer, and cook for 1 hour. Strain
and let cool. Cover and refrigerate for up to 3 days.

WILD MUSHROOM RISOTTO

This is my idea of comfort food; it's gotten our family through
many a Sunday evening in winter, accompanied with any of
several fresh and fruity reds.

> ⊰ wine recommendation: pinot noir, morgon, julienas,
> fleurie, chinon ⊱

> 2 OUNCES DRIED PORCINI MUSHROOMS
>
> 2 CUPS BOILING WATER
>
> 8 CUPS VEGETABLE BROTH (see previous recipe)
>
> 2 TABLESPOONS EXTRA-VIRGIN OLIVE OIL
>
> 1 ONION, FINELY CHOPPED
>
> 4 OUNCES FRESH MUSHROOMS, CHOPPED
>
> 2 CUPS ARBORIO RICE
>
> 1 CUP DRY WHITE WINE
>
> 2 TABLESPOONS FRESHLY GRATED PARMESAN CHEESE

Serves four as a main course

~Put the dried mushrooms in a medium bowl and pour the boiling
water over. Let stand for 20 minutes. Remove the mushrooms
and squeeze dry over the bowl, reserving the liquid. Chop coarsely
and set aside. In a medium saucepan, bring the broth to a low
simmer. Add 1 cup of the mushroom water.

~In a medium, heavy pan, heat the oil over medium heat. Add
the onion and cook until translucent, about 3 minutes. Stir in the
fresh mushrooms. Add the rice and stir until opaque, 2 to 3
minutes. Add the wine and cook, stirring constantly, until almost
evaporated. Add half the reconstituted dried mushrooms to the
pan. Stir in the broth ½ cup at a time, stirring frequently until
each addition of liquid is absorbed. After about 20 minutes, test
for doneness; the rice should be firm but tender. If not, add
another ½ cup of broth or water, and cook for 1 or 2 more
minutes. Add the rest of the reconstituted mushrooms and stir
in the cheese. Serve in warmed shallow bowls.

POULTRY

Chicken and turkey, by themselves, don't invite too many immediate associations with wine—they're a little too bland and unassertive, pretty much the wallflowers at the banquet table. They are, however, easily transformed, not only by herbs and spices and marinades and sauces, but also by cooking methods, so that in many ways they're more amenable and flexible partners than meat or fish.

The most important thing about matching chicken and wine is to consider how the birds will be flavored and cooked, and the formality (or lack of it) of the occasion. The occasion also matters a lot with turkey, as that bird is usually the center-piece of a large holiday meal, surrounded by an array of vegetables and garnishes, as well as the inevitable gravy. Guinea hen, which is usually farmed these days, also falls into the unassertive category, as does Cornish hen. Dark-meat birds like duck, quail, goose, and squab have enough character to be easier matches, as do game birds like pheasant.

For most preparations of chicken, either red or white wine will do at least half the time, as long as the wines aren't too heavy or assertive. Light, fruity reds like Beaujolais, Valpolicella, most Merlots, Dolcetto, and Pinot Noir generally work best, while German and Alsatian Riesling, Pinot Gris, Viognier, and good-quality Chenin Blanc or Sancerre are good bets. Basically, think like for like: fragrantly aromatic dishes with spices such as Chinese five-spice powder or herbs like lemon thyme go well with Viognier, or Beaujolais if you prefer red, while dishes like barbecued chicken will work best with a fruity yet lightly acidic white like Riesling, or a lightly tannic red like Dolcetto or Merlot. With roasts, you need to consider the stuffing and spices and basting liquid, but the firm texture of the meat might prompt you to step up a notch to a slightly more assertive wine; for something like roast capon basted with butter, for example, match rich with rich and go for Chardonnay.

Turkey prompts the most questions in any wine writer's mail bag every year. Not only are there the various vegetables—the sweet potatoes, the Brussels sprouts, the mashed potatoes, the peas, and all those variables—but there are the two kinds of cranberry sauce and the pan gravy, and there are often regional specialties like fried okra and other exotic greens. Then there's the white-and-dark-meat problem, and then there's Aunt Harriet, who only likes sweet white wine, and Uncle Harry, who only drinks red. The advice most often given is to put out several different bottles and let people choose for themselves, but that's neither gracious nor seemly—there's enough to talk about without a wine debate. Accept the fact that if there is a fairly large group and a fairly large menu, everything is going to be something of a compromise, and put out just two kinds of wine, white and red, of medium body and acidity and dryness, as good as you can afford and the company deserves.

Turkey also seems like the best place to mention the matter of leftovers: Cold meat of all sorts, but especially chicken and turkey, are quite wonderful with German Riesling; the fruitiness and lively acidity of the wine gives the meat a nice lift. The same goes for chicken salad, as long as it's not overdressed with vinaigrette or mayo. Chicken hash is a great partner for dry Alsatian Riesling, a classic bistro combination.

Duck is pretty much of a no-brainer: very good red Burgundy or Pinot Noir or Syrah, unless you're making one of those French recipes where the duck is drenched in fruit sauces (in which case Cabernet Sauvignon might cut through better), or Chinese or Thai style, where the best compromise is a cooled fruity light red. Classic choices for goose tend to be regional, with very, very good German Riesling getting the nod, but I still prefer very good red Burgundy or Pinot Noir for goose as well as quail, because the meat is fairly succulent and only slightly dark. Squab, which is really pigeon, has very dark, dense flesh and works best with a fine, full red like well-matured Cabernet Sauvignon or red Bordeaux, or older Zinfandel.

GRILLED ORANGE-MUSTARD CHICKEN THIGHS

Dark-meat thighs have more flavor than breasts and cook through more easily, especially if the bone is left in. Be sure to trim the skin and as much fat as possible from around the edges, to avoid flare-ups from the fire as the fat melts. This marinade is actually fairly light, and the best match, light, crisp, and refreshing, comes from Germany, one of the best food wines of summer.

◦{wine recommendation: riesling}◦

Serves eight

¼ CUP OLIVE OIL

¼ CUP FRESH ORANGE JUICE

3 TABLESPOONS DIJON MUSTARD

3 TABLESPOONS ORANGE MARMALADE

2 TABLESPOONS HONEY

4 CLOVES GARLIC, MINCED

1 TABLESPOON CHOPPED FRESH TARRAGON

1 TEASPOON FRESHLY GROUND PEPPER

8 CHICKEN THIGHS

~In a large bowl, whisk together all the ingredients except the chicken. Add the chicken, cover, and refrigerate for at least 6 hours or overnight.

~Light a fire in a charcoal grill. Remove the chicken from the refrigerator 30 minutes before cooking. Remove the chicken from the marinade. Put the chicken, skin-side up, on a lightly greased grill rack and turn twice in the first few minutes to brown both sides evenly, then alternately at 5-minute intervals for a total of about 30 minutes. Have the remainder of the marinade handy in a small pot and brush the chicken pieces after turning each time for the first 20 minutes, then discard what's left. Or, preheat the broiler. Place the chicken on a broiler pan lined with aluminum foil and broil 4 inches from the heat source for 20 minutes, turning and basting twice in the first 10 minutes, and finishing skin-side up. Test for doneness: Juices should run quite clear when a thigh is pierced. The chicken should be quite well browned on the outside but juicy inside.

COQ AU VIN

This is a classic dish from Burgundy, but one that's been fiddled with almost beyond recognition—perhaps it seems too simple for cooks with something to prove. Old-time Burgundian cooks used to insist this dish had to be made with a rooster, and that his blood be stirred into the sauce, but there I part company with tradition; the best free-range chicken available is fine. It was always made with red wine, too, and that really does provide a better, fuller flavor (I was once served a version of this dish made with Lancer's rosé, which is as far to the other extreme as you can get—it was ghostly, like a faded old photograph). In the pot, you can economize with a Côtes-du-Rhône, but don't settle for less than the best in your glass.

{wine recommendation: burgundy, or california or oregon pinot noir}

Serves six

2 TABLESPOONS OLIVE OIL
18 SHALLOTS
4 SLICES BACON, CHOPPED
1 CHICKEN, ABOUT 4 POUNDS, CUT INTO SERVING PIECES
SALT AND FRESHLY GROUND PEPPER TO TASTE
1 TABLESPOON FLOUR
¼ CUP BRANDY
1 BOTTLE (750 ml) DRY RED WINE
2 BAY LEAVES
1 SPRIG THYME
3 CLOVES GARLIC
8 OUNCES MUSHROOMS, HALVED
BUTTERED EGG NOODLES FOR SERVING

~Preheat the oven to 325°F. In a heavy casserole or Dutch oven large enough to hold the chicken, heat the oil over medium heat. Add the shallots and bacon, and cook for about 10 minutes, or until lightly browned. Using a slotted spoon, transfer to a plate and set aside. Add the chicken pieces and brown on all sides. Add the salt and pepper. Sprinkle with the flour. Heat the brandy in a small pan and pour it over the chicken. Using a long-handled match—which is not only safer but helps to improve the flavor—light the brandy. When the flames subside, stir well to scrape up the browned bits from the bottom of the pan. Add the shallots and bacon, wine, herbs, and garlic. Bring to a simmer, cover, and bake for 1 hour.

~Using a slotted spoon, transfer the chicken and shallots to a heated plate and cover loosely with aluminum foil. Strain the pan liquids through a fine-mesh sieve into a bowl, pressing on the solids with the back of a large spoon. Discard the solids. Return the liquid to the pan and cook over medium heat to reduce it by about a third. Reduce the heat to a simmer. Add the chicken, shallots, and mushrooms. Cook for about 10 minutes, uncovered. Serve over noodles.

ALSATIAN CHICKEN IN RIESLING SAUCE

Part of my family was from Alsace, in northern France, but what finally drew me there was gastronomy, not nostalgia: Alsatians are heroic and sophisticated cooks, and their wines are superb. These people don't hold back in the kitchen, and they tend to cook with their best wines. For this classic, I would say that you should do the same. Corners can often be cut on wine in the pot, but this dish just isn't the same without a good, dry Alsatian Riesling. Though there is cream in this dish, an ingredient that seems to have been banished from menus everywhere but in Alsace, it's still fairly light. The perfect match in your glass is obvious.

◦{wine recommendation: riesling}◦

Serves six

4 TABLESPOONS UNSALTED BUTTER

1 TABLESPOON OLIVE OIL

1 CHICKEN, ABOUT 4 POUNDS, CUT INTO SERVING PIECES

1 ONION, FINELY CHOPPED

4 OUNCES MUSHROOMS, SLICED

3 TABLESPOONS BRANDY

1 BAY LEAF

2 CUPS RIESLING AT ROOM TEMPERATURE

¾ CUP HEAVY CREAM AT ROOM TEMPERATURE

BUTTERED EGG NOODLES FOR SERVING

~In a large, heavy skillet, melt the butter with the oil over medium heat and brown the chicken pieces on all sides. Stir in the onion and mushrooms. Heat the brandy in a small pan and pour over the chicken. Using a long-handled match, light the brandy; stir until the flames subside. Add the bay leaf and wine. Bring to a simmer, cover, and cook gently for 30 minutes, or until the chicken is tender.

~Using a slotted spoon, transfer the chicken to a heated plate and cover loosely with aluminum foil. Remove and discard the bay leaf. Stir in the cream and increase heat to a low boil. Cook, stirring constantly, for about 5 minutes. Reduce heat, return the chicken to the sauce and cook, uncovered, for 10 minutes. Serve over warm noodles.

BLUE CHEESE ROAST CHICKEN WITH APPLE-THYME STUFFING

This is the easiest elegant dish I know. The preparation is quite hands-on, but it only takes a few minutes and creates a deliciously complex combination of flavors. The roasting technique is the best way to get a gorgeous brown bird, uniformly cooked through. Given the richness and complexity of this dish, the best companion needs to be the same.

⊰wine recommendation: chardonnay⊱

Serves six

2 TABLESPOONS UNSALTED BUTTER, PLUS ½ CUP (1 stick) UNSALTED BUTTER AT ROOM TEMPERATURE

3 GRANNY SMITH APPLES, PEELED, CORED, AND CUT INTO ½-INCH CHUNKS

3 SHALLOTS, COARSELY CHOPPED

1 STALK CELERY, FINELY CHOPPED

1 TABLESPOON MINCED FRESH THYME

1 BAY LEAF

4 OUNCES BLUE CHEESE, CRUMBLED

1 ROASTING CHICKEN, ABOUT 5 POUNDS

1 TABLESPOON OLIVE OIL

~Preheat the oven to 425°F. In a large skillet, melt the 2 tablespoons butter over medium-low heat. Add the apples, shallots, celery, and thyme and sauté for 7 or 8 minutes, or until browned (this is to intensify the flavor; try not to mash the apples). Transfer to a bowl and add the bay leaf.

~In a small bowl, cream the ½ cup butter and the cheese together. Loosen the skin of the chicken across the breast, beginning at the back of the bird, by inserting a finger under the skin and then running it back and forth, side to side, then forward. Make a small cut in the skin at the end of each leg and run a finger around the meat. Take chunks of the butter mixture and insert it under the skin. Knead the mixture forward by rubbing the skin until there is a layer of the mixture across the breast and thigh meat (don't worry if it's a bit lumpy—it'll melt down and into the meat). Whisk the olive oil with a little of the remaining butter mixture and rub it into the outside of the skin across the breast and top of the thigh. Stuff the bird with the apple mixture and tie the legs together with cotton twine.

~Put the chicken on its side on a rack in a baking dish. Roast, uncovered, for 20 minutes. Turn onto its other side, baste, and roast 20 minutes longer. Turn the chicken breast-side up, baste, and roast for another 20 minutes. Lower the oven temperature to 375°F, baste, and roast for about 15 more minutes, or until juices run clear when a thigh is pierced.

~Turn the oven off. Remove the chicken from the oven and place it, breast-side down, on a platter. Cover loosely with aluminum foil and return to the oven, but leave the door partly open (this allows the meat to rest and firm up, and the juices to flow around it). Let rest for 15 minutes. Carve by removing the entire half-breast from each side and cutting it into lengthwise slices so that everyone gets some crispy skin. Carve off the legs. Return the sliced meat and legs to the warm platter and serve.

SAUTÉED CHICKEN AND ARTICHOKE HEARTS

This is a modern version of an old San Francisco dish called, for reasons no one can remember for sure, Chicken Jerusalem. It's rustic, but the flavors are direct, intense, and robust. Despite the presence of artichokes (see "What's the Problem?," page 30), this dish is reasonably wine-friendly, partly because the artichokes aren't freshly cooked and are therefore lower in the acid that changes wine's flavor, and also because the wine I favor is New Zealand or California Sauvignon Blanc, which has a fairly high level of acidity, so the wine can hold its own. In the pan, use any inexpensive but palatable dry white wine, such as the various French Vins de Pays d'Oc.

◦{wine recommendation: sauvignon blanc }◦

Serves eight

2 TABLESPOONS UNSALTED BUTTER

2 TABLESPOONS OLIVE OIL

2 SMALL CHICKENS (about 2½ pounds each), CUT INTO SERVING PIECES AND SKINNED

SALT AND FRESHLY GROUND PEPPER TO TASTE

3 ONIONS, COARSELY CHOPPED

4 CLOVES GARLIC, MINCED

1 LARGE RED BELL PEPPER, ROASTED, PEELED, AND CUT INTO STRIPS (see page 62)

1 TABLESPOON FRESH TARRAGON, CHOPPED

1 CUP DRY WHITE WINE

¾ CUP CANNED LOW-SALT CHICKEN BROTH

1 EIGHT-OUNCE JAR OIL-MARINATED ARTICHOKE HEARTS, DRAINED

8 OUNCES MUSHROOMS, QUARTERED

STEAMED LONG-GRAIN WHITE RICE FOR SERVING

~In a large, heavy casserole or Dutch oven wide enough to hold the chicken in one layer, melt the butter with the oil over medium heat. Sprinkle the chicken pieces with salt and pepper and brown for 2 or 3 minutes on each side. Remove the chicken and sauté the onions and garlic in the pan for about 5 minutes, or until golden. Add the red bell pepper, tarragon, and wine. Increase heat to a rapid simmer and cook for 5 minutes, stirring to scrape up any browned bits from the bottom of the pan. Return the chicken to the pan. Add the chicken broth, cover, reduce heat to a simmer, and cook for 10 minutes.

~Add the artichoke hearts and mushrooms. Stir well, cover, and simmer for 10 minutes. To serve, remove the chicken and vegetables with a slotted spoon, placing them on a bed of steamed rice on each of 8 warmed plates. Increase heat to high and boil the pan juices, stirring constantly, until they're reduced to a thick, syrupy consistency. Pour over the chicken.

HAZELNUT CHICKEN BREASTS WITH DIJON-YOGURT SAUCE

John Sarich is a distinguished chef in Seattle, and the culinary director of Château Ste. Michelle, one of Washington state's leading wineries. At one lunch there, he served this dish, adapted from a recipe he first tried in Dijon, which is in Burgundy. It's quick, easy, and has a nice refreshing bite under the richness of the topping. I like the way he substitutes yogurt for the cream in the original—I've tried it both ways, and this is better.

⊰{wine recommendation: chardonnay}⊱

Serves six

6 BONELESS, SKINLESS CHICKEN BREAST HALVES

1 CUP HAZELNUTS, TOASTED, SKINNED, AND FINELY CHOPPED (see Note, page 66)

2 TABLESPOONS UNSALTED BUTTER, AT ROOM TEMPERATURE

2 LARGE SHALLOTS, MINCED

2 TABLESPOONS PLAIN YOGURT

1 TABLESPOON MINCED FRESH TARRAGON

1 TABLESPOON DIJON MUSTARD

1 TABLESPOON DRY WHITE WINE

SALT AND FRESHLY GROUND PEPPER TO TASTE

SAUCE:

2 CUPS PLAIN YOGURT, AT ROOM TEMPERATURE

1 TABLESPOON DIJON MUSTARD

1 TEASPOON SUGAR

1/2 TEASPOON GRATED LEMON ZEST

1 TABLESPOON FRESH LEMON JUICE

1/4 CUP DRY WHITE WINE

SALT AND FRESHLY GROUND PEPPER TO TASTE

~Preheat the oven to 350°F. Put the chicken breasts in an oiled baking pan. In a small bowl, mix the hazelnuts, butter, shallots, yogurt, tarragon, mustard, wine, salt, and pepper together. Spread the mixture evenly over the chicken breasts. Bake for 20 minutes, or until opaque throughout.

~Meanwhile, whisk the sauce ingredients together. To serve, spoon the sauce onto warmed plates and top with the chicken breasts.

SESAME CHICKEN SALAD

I love the nutty, distinctive flavor and aroma of sesame oil—its assertiveness is definite but good-natured, which is why it goes so well with dishes like steamed fish, which only need a subtle boost. It's even better with chicken, and that smooth nuttiness takes it into easy complicity with wine.

{wine recommendation: sauvignon blanc, budget (unoaked) chardonnay }

Serves four

4 BONELESS, SKINLESS CHICKEN BREASTS, CUT INTO BITE-SIZED CHUNKS

2 TABLESPOONS ASIAN SESAME OIL

1 LARGE CLOVE GARLIC, MINCED

1 TABLESPOON SESAME SEEDS

DRESSING:

1 TABLESPOON PINE NUTS

4 TABLESPOONS ASIAN SESAME OIL

2 TABLESPOONS FRESH LEMON JUICE

1 TEASPOON SOY SAUCE

1-INCH SQUARE FRESH GINGER, PEELED AND CHOPPED

LEAVES FROM 4 SPRIGS OF CILANTRO

2 TABLESPOONS DRY WHITE WINE

LEAVES FROM 1 HEAD RED-LEAF LETTUCE, TORN INTO PIECES

4 OR 5 LEAVES ICEBERG LETTUCE, CUT INTO THIN STRIPS

1 YELLOW BELL PEPPER, SEEDED, DERIBBED, AND CUT INTO THIN STRIPS

4 ROMA (plum) TOMATOES, PEELED, SEEDED, AND CUT INTO STRIPS

2 TABLESPOONS PINE NUTS, TOASTED

~Put the chicken in a bowl, and add the sesame oil and garlic. Toss to coat well, cover, and refrigerate for at least 2 hours or up to 4 hours.

~Soak 4 medium-length wooden skewers in water for at least 30 minutes. Preheat the broiler. Brush the garlic bits off the chicken pieces, drain the skewers, and thread the chicken on them. Broil 4 inches from the heat source for 4 minutes on the first side, then 2 minutes on the second side, or until browned on the outside and opaque throughout. Remove from heat and sprinkle with the sesame seeds. Set aside.

~To make the dressing: In a blender or food processor, combine all the ingredients and process until smooth.

~In a large bowl, combine the lettuce, bell pepper, and tomatoes. Toss with half the dressing, and divide among 4 plates. Sprinkle the 2 tablespoons pine nuts on top. Remove the chicken from the skewers and arrange over the salad. Drizzle the remaining dressing over the chicken.

GREEN CURRY CHICKEN

This recipe demonstrates the importance of tasting with an open mind. I was visited last year by a wine maker from the southern Rhône, and we decided to have a quick lunch together. There's a Thai restaurant downstairs from the *Decanter* offices, and he suggested that as a possibility. I demurred, as we'd planned to taste his red wines and I didn't think hot and spicy food might match them. He laughed and insisted. We ate several spicy dishes, including curries, we tasted his voluptuous, soft red wines from Gigondas, Vacqueyras, and Côtes-du-Rhône Villages, and I enjoyed the delicious revelation that they matched the food beautifully (as would good Beaujolais, I later discovered). You can prove it with this easy, moderately hot green curry from the Chiang Mai Thai Cookery School, run by Somphon Nabnian in Thailand, where I wish we'd known about the wine match at the time. Chill the wine lightly for about 30 minutes in the fridge. Most Thai restaurants don't have great wine lists, but it would be worth inquiring about bringing your own wine and paying a few dollars corkage, rather than ruining the meal with beer.

{wine recommendation: gigondas, beaujolais}

Serves six

1 TABLESPOON CORN OR PEANUT OIL

2 TABLESPOONS THAI GREEN CURRY PASTE*

3 CUPS COCONUT MILK*

1 POUND BONELESS, SKINLESS CHICKEN BREASTS, SLICED THINLY ACROSS

2 EGGPLANTS, CUT INTO ½-INCH CHUNKS

8 OUNCES THAWED FROZEN PEAS

2 TABLESPOONS FISH SAUCE*

2 KAFFIR LIME LEAVES*, OR 2 BAY LEAVES AND A SQUEEZE OF LIME

STEAMED RICE FOR SERVING

1 RED THAI CHILI, CUT INTO THIN CROSSWISE SLICES

12 FRESH BASIL LEAVES, TORN IN HALF

~Heat the oil in a wok or large skillet over medium-high heat. Add the curry paste and a few tablespoons of the coconut milk, to keep the paste from spattering. Stir and cook for 3 or 4 minutes, to bring out the flavor. Add the chicken, stir well, and cook for 4 or 5 minutes, stirring all the while. Add the remaining coconut milk. Bring to a rapid simmer. Add the eggplant, peas, fish sauce, and lime leaves. Stir well. Simmer for 5 minutes, and serve over steamed rice, garnished with the chili and the basil leaves.

Available at Asian markets, or in the Asian-food section of many large supermarkets.

CORNISH HENS EN COCOTTE

My favorite cooking pot is made of glazed terra-cotta; it's called an *olla,* and I dragged it back from Spain as hand luggage before I found out I could have bought one just as cheaply at home, at Pier One Imports. It's the original nonstick utensil, it heats evenly in the oven or on the stove top (I use a heat-diffusion screen over a gas flame), and of course is nonreactive, so acidic food like tomatoes and citrus fruits keep their flavor perfectly. Any medium-sized casserole or Dutch oven will do for this recipe, though. I also got the idea for this dish in Spain, where they drink red with almost everything.

{wine recommendation: rioja}

Serves four

2 CORNISH HENS

1 TABLESPOON OLIVE OIL

2 SLICES BACON, DICED

3 TABLESPOONS BRANDY

½ CUP DRY WHITE WINE

½ CUP CANNED LOW-SALT CHICKEN BROTH

3 SPRIGS THYME

2 TABLESPOONS UNSALTED BUTTER

8 OUNCES CREMINI MUSHROOMS

2 TABLESPOONS MINCED FRESH PARSLEY

~Preheat the oven to 325°F. Remove the hens from the refrigerator 30 minutes before baking.

~In a heavy casserole or Dutch oven, heat the oil over medium heat. Add the bacon and cook until it begins to brown. Add the hens and cook, turning to brown lightly on all sides. Add the brandy, wine, broth, and thyme. Cover tightly (a good trick is to fold a large sheet of aluminum foil in half, put it over the top of the casserole, then put the cover on that, pressing down—it makes a good seal). Bring to a boil—you'll hear it bubble. Place in the oven and bake for 1 hour, or until the juices run clear when a thigh is pierced.

~After about 45 minutes, melt the butter in a small pan over medium-low heat and cook the mushrooms for 15 minutes, or until browned. Add the parsley and set aside.

~Remove the hens from the pan and keep warm. Add the mushrooms, parsley, and butter to the pan, increase heat to medium-high, and stir well to scrape up any browned bits from the bottom of the pan. Split the hens in half by cutting down the backs, then down the breasts. Serve ½ hen per person, with the sauce poured over.

ROAST TURKEY STUFFED WITH PANCETTA AND HERBS

Italians took to turkey as no other European nation did, probably because they saw the bird the way artists see blank spaces, as something to project their imagination and ego onto. (The French were more reluctant, even doubting the bird's origins. French gourmet Brillat-Savarin said it had to have come from America: "Note the appearance of the bird, which is clearly outlandish.") In Italy, you see it on menus of even the most exalted restaurants, sliced and stuffed with a spicy filling, poached lightly in flavored olive oil, roasted and stuffed with chestnuts, or braised in wine to a juicy tenderness. The idea that anyone would eat such a magnificent food only twice a year, and pretty much the same way each time, with the same side dishes, would seem like absurd self-denial.

The Thanksgiving and Christmas turkey always brings up the problem of what wine to serve with it. The breast is bland and white, the legs dark; the cranberry sauce is sweet; the Brussels sprouts or broccoli are sulfurous; and the giblet gravy is rich. I'd serve a light, fairly dry but fruity red like Merlot or Beaujolais, and a Riesling and middle-of-the-road Chardonnay, not too expensive. Then, some other time, when you have like-minded friends over, serve this Italianate roast turkey with middleweight reds.

⊰ wine recommendation: valpolicella superiore, chianti, zinfandel ⊱

1 TURKEY, 10 TO 12 POUNDS

SALT TO TASTE

2 TABLESPOONS OLIVE OIL, PLUS MORE FOR COATING

1 ONION, FINELY CHOPPED

4 CLOVES GARLIC, MINCED

1 POUND GROUND PORK

8 OUNCES SWEET ITALIAN SAUSAGE, REMOVED FROM CASING

2 CUPS LOOSELY PACKED CUBED SOURDOUGH BREAD, WITHOUT CRUSTS, SOAKED IN ½ CUP DRY WHITE WINE

1 TABLESPOON MINCED FRESH SAGE

1 TABLESPOON MINCED FRESH THYME

1 TABLESPOON MINCED FRESH BASIL

3 TABLESPOONS PINE NUTS

½ CUP (2 ounces) FRESHLY GRATED PARMESAN CHEESE

3 TABLESPOONS MEDIUM-SWEET MARSALA WINE

3 TABLESPOONS MINCED FRESH ROSEMARY

3 OUNCES PANCETTA, FINELY CHOPPED

FRESHLY GROUND PEPPER TO TASTE

Serves twelve

~Preheat the oven to 350°F. Rinse and dry the turkey. Rub the inside with salt.

~Heat 1 tablespoon of the oil in a medium-large skillet and sauté the onion and half the garlic for about 5 minutes, or until soft. Add the pork and sausage meat. Cook for about 10 minutes, stirring well, until it loses its raw pink color. Remove from heat and let cool.

~Meanwhile, in a large bowl, combine the bread cubes, herbs, pine nuts, Parmesan, and Marsala. Add the meat and mix well. Set aside. In a small bowl, combine the rosemary, pancetta, and remaining garlic. Mix well. Loosen the skin of the turkey across the breast, beginning at the back of the bird, by inserting a finger under the skin and running it back and forth, side to side, then forward. Insert the rosemary mixture under the skin and massage it around forward fairly evenly across the breast meat (it will provide an aromatic, delicious self-baste). Stuff the turkey and skewer the cavity closed.

~Place the bird on a rack in a roasting pan and brush or rub the skin liberally with olive oil, then rub with salt and pepper. Roast, basting occasionally with more olive oil, for about 3 hours (figuring 18 minutes to the pound), or until juices run clear when a thigh is pricked. Remove from the oven, let rest for 10 minutes, and carve.

GRILLED QUAIL IN GINGER-PORT MARINADE

Fortified wines like port, sherry, and Madeira have been classic bases for meat sauces and marinades for a long time, especially for strong-flavored meats like beef and venison, but they do equally well with dark-meat birds like duck and quail when livened up with the right spices. Here, I've combined ginger and star anise (available in Asian markets and supermarkets) to give a slightly hot and spicy edge to a marinade. The port can be a simple generic version from Portugal, not expensive—the idea is simply to take advantage of its basic character, which gives the birds a slightly sweet, unusual flavor. The best wine partner is a light but firm red that combines a touch of spiciness and fruitiness, but is assertive enough to hold its own.

{wine recommendation: pinot noir, chianti classico}

Serves four

MARINADE:

2 TABLESPOONS OLIVE OIL

2 SHALLOTS, MINCED

1-INCH SQUARE FRESH GINGER, MINCED

$\frac{1}{2}$ TEASPOON FRESHLY GROUND PEPPER

3 STAR ANISE PODS, WHOLE

1 CUP PORT

8 QUAIL

~To make the marinade: Heat the oil in small saucepan over medium heat and sauté the shallots, ginger, pepper, and star anise for 2 minutes. Add the port and simmer for 5 minutes. Remove from heat.

~Cut the backbones out of the quail and put the birds on a cutting board, breast-side up. Press down on the breasts to flatten each one. Run bamboo skewers sideways through each leg and through the upper body under the wings to hold the birds flat. (If you will be grilling them in a grill basket, skip this step.) Put the quail in a large baking pan in one layer and add the marinade. Cover and refrigerate for at least 4 hours or overnight.

~Remove the quail from the marinade. Light a fire in a charcoal grill or preheat the broiler. In a small saucepan, boil the marinade for 5 minutes. Grill or broil the quail about 4 minutes on each side, basting with the marinade after turning.

ROAST DUCKLING WITH ASIAN SPICES

Roast duck with fruit is a fine French idea at the table—delicious. In the kitchen, however, it can be a complicated business, with usually at least three fairly complicated steps, and a lot of different theories about how best to actually cook the bird. There is an easier way, I've found: this one-step, slow-cooking method, which yields a tender, crispy-skinned duck. There is no sauce, and fruit is not involved; one way to balance the duck's richness is to serve it with mashed sweet potatoes, or a German dish called "heaven and earth," which is boiled potatoes and apples coarsely mashed together. The glaze may seem a bit pungent, but once it cooks in and mingles with the juices, it's just nicely spicy.

The wine needs to have some power, and certainly good acidity, and should be a little gamey or funky; most Zinfandel, for example, is too fruity and smooth, and Merlot too soft. The perfect match needs a cutting edge.

{wine recommendation: oregon or california pinot noir, washington or california syrah}

Serves two	4 BAY LEAVES
	1 DUCKLING, ABOUT 4 POUNDS
	3 GARLIC CLOVES, MINCED
	½ TEASPOON FRESHLY GROUND PEPPER
	2 TEASPOONS CHINESE FIVE-SPICE POWDER*
	MINCED ZEST OF 1 ORANGE
	2 TABLESPOONS DARK SOY SAUCE OR TAMARI SAUCE
	2 TABLESPOONS HONEY
	12 WHOLE CLOVES

~Preheat oven to 425°F. Put bay leaves inside the duck.

~In a small bowl, whisk together all the remaining ingredients except the cloves. Or, puree them in a blender, for a smoother mixture. Brush or rub the syrupy mixture evenly all over the duck. With the point of a small paring knife, make 2 rows of 6 incisions along the top of the duck's breast, right into the meat, and insert a clove in each. Place the duck on a rack in a roasting pan lined with aluminum foil.

~Roast the duck for 20 minutes, then reduce the oven temperature to 350°F. Roast for 2 more hours, occasionally pouring off any excess fat, which otherwise might spatter. (If the glaze begins to scorch, cover loosely with aluminum foil.)

~Remove from the oven and cut away the duck legs to check for doneness: The dark meat may still be too rare, showing a reddish tinge. If so, put the legs back in the oven for 5 minutes, while the rest of the duck rests. Disjoint and serve the legs alongside the carved breasts, from which the cloves have been removed.

*Available at Asian markets, or in the Asian-food section of many large supermarkets.

FISH AND SHELLFISH

The only non-Spaniard I ever knew who preferred red wine with fish was the late San Francisco newspaper columnist Charles McCabe, but then he reveled in being known as "the Great Dissenter." For the rest of us, it's white wine with fish, at least most of the time, and with good reason: There's simply more sheer synergy springing out of the right white match than with almost any other pairing. The best qualities of the right white—its crisp acidity, subtle fruit, lightness or fullness, and its coolness—all combine to boost and define the flavor of fish, but even more importantly, the right fish brings out all the nuances of the wine. At their best, the combination is like two great dancers in motion, beautifully synchronized.

The ideal balance here is struck between the acidity in the wine and the richness or oiliness in the fish, and by matching the relative weight and texture of each: Pinot Grigio, Riesling, or Soave with flaky white fish, for example; a tart middleweight like Semillon or Sauvignon Blanc with swordfish, snapper, or grouper; and your best white Burgundy, or Carneros or Margaret River Chardonnay, with scallops, lobster, sole, or halibut. On the other hand, some meaty fish like tuna, and salmon sometimes, go nicely with a light red like Burgundy, Beaujolais, Gigondas, or Pinot Noir, if it's not too tannic—in most simple preparations, tannin tends to give fish a metallic aftertaste.

There are exceptions, mainly some classic preparations where fish is cooked in red wine, which brings its flavor around to easy compatibility. In the Loire Valley, freshwater fish and shellfish are often simmered in the local light Chinon or Bourgeuil, and in Bordeaux, which has access to ocean fish as well, monkfish is cut into scallops and simmered in a casserole with the local reds. In northeastern Italy, they're just close enough to the Mediterranean to have access to sea bass, which they sometimes roast and baste with a strong red. In Rioja, they bake a common and rather ugly fish called hake in the local wine, which elevates its status far above its real worth. If you like fish, these are all delicious alternatives to the usual methods. In each case, drink the same wine you cook with, but lightly chilled, say 30 minutes, in the fridge, just enough to take the edge off its room-temperature warmth.

THYME-INFUSED SEARED SCALLOPS AND MORELS

Shellfish love wine, and the feeling's mutual; there's just some extra affinity at work that makes even simple meals seem special. Which of course means that when you put together a special dinner, a good wine and shellfish combination covers a lot of extra distance. This dish has the additional virtue of being easy, but it has so much flavor and richness that it demands the best of white wines, such as a pricey white Burgundy like Corton-Charlemagne or Montrachet, or California Chardonnay from Carneros, the Russian River Valley, or the Santa Maria Valley in Santa Barbara County. Like morels, they (and we) are worth splurging on.

◦{ wine recommendation: the best chardonnay }◦

Serves six

1 TABLESPOON EXTRA-VIRGIN OLIVE OIL

1½ POUNDS SEA SCALLOPS (about 24)

1½ TABLESPOONS MINCED FRESH THYME

2 OUNCES DRIED MORELS

12 OIL-PACKED SUN-DRIED TOMATOES DRAINED AND FINELY CHOPPED

2 SHALLOTS, MINCED

1 CLOVE GARLIC, MINCED

1 SPRIG THYME

¼ CUP DRY WHITE WINE

1 TABLESPOON UNSALTED BUTTER

SALT AND FRESHLY GROUND PEPPER TO TASTE

~Pour the olive oil onto a platter and place the scallops on it in one layer. Turn them over to coat with oil and sprinkle half the thyme evenly over them. Turn again and sprinkle the remaining thyme over. Cover the plate with plastic wrap and refrigerate for 1 hour.

~Soak the morels in hot water to cover for 30 minutes. Drain, pat dry, and cut in half lengthwise. Put in a small bowl with the sun-dried tomato pieces.

~Remove the scallops from the refrigerator 30 minutes before cooking. In a small saucepan, combine the shallots, garlic, thyme sprig, and wine. Bring to a simmer and cook to reduce by half. Remove the thyme. Add the morels and tomatoes, and whisk the butter into the sauce. Season with salt and pepper and keep warm.

~Heat 2 large nonstick skillets over high heat until hot (if you have only 1 skillet, cook the scallops in batches). In one layer and not crowded, cook the scallops until lightly browned on the outside and just opaque throughout, no more than 2 minutes on each side. (The light oil covering of the marinade is all the cooking liquid they'll need.) Transfer the scallops to a warmed bowl. Pour the sauce over, mixing gently, and cover the bowl for 2 or 3 minutes to let the scallops soak up the sauce.

CHILLED SALMON WITH ASIAN VINAIGRETTE

This is the simplest elegant buffet dish I know of, and a real time-saver, as it's made ahead. Basically, the fillet is steamed, which gives it a wonderful firm texture and allows the spices to soak in and infuse it with considerable extra flavor, and then it's lightly chilled. This dish also works well as an appetizer for a formal meal. In that instance, cook less fish, slice the fillet into 2-inch-wide pieces crosswise, and place them on a bed of arugula or mixed greens with some diced cucumber on top. The vinaigrette is very mild because of the rice vinegar, and won't get in the way of the wine, which should be crisp and bracing.

⊰wine recommendation: california sauvignon blanc, pouilly-fumé⊱

*Serves sixteen
as appetizer
or as part of
a buffet*

1 TEASPOON FRESHLY GROUND PEPPER

1 TEASPOON WHOLE CARDAMOM PODS

1 TEASPOON STAR ANISE PODS

1 TEASPOON CORIANDER SEEDS

1 SALMON FILLET, ABOUT 2 POUNDS, SKIN AND PIN BONES REMOVED

1 CUCUMBER, CUT INTO VERY THIN SLICES

1 GREEN BELL PEPPER, SEEDED, DERIBBED, AND DICED

¼ CUP WALNUT OIL

2 TABLESPOONS RICE VINEGAR

LARGE PINCH OF PAPRIKA

SALT AND FRESHLY GROUND PEPPER TO TASTE

~In a mortar or spice grinder, combine the ground pepper, cardamom, star anise, and coriander, and crush or grind to a powder. Reserve ¼ teaspoon of the mixture for the vinaigrette, and rub the rest into the top of the fillet. Place in a covered steamer over briskly simmering water and steam for 5 minutes. Remove, let cool, and refrigerate for at least 30 minutes or up to 1 hour.

~Make a bed of thin cucumber slices on a platter. With a very sharp knife, cut the salmon into 1-inch crosswise slices. Arrange the pieces in a row on the cucumber, which should be showing beneath the edges of the fillet. Scatter the diced bell pepper on top. Blend the walnut oil, vinegar, paprika, salt, pepper, and remaining spice mixture together and drizzle over the top.

TROUT POACHED IN CHAMPAGNE

In the Champagne district of France, quite a few dishes consist of fish or poultry poached or braised in the local wine—lucky Champenois! Jamie Davies, doyenne of Schramsberg Vineyards in the Napa Valley, has come up with one of the best variations on this idea, with a nice American twist in the creamy avocado sauce. This is an elegant first course; use the same Champagne in the sauce that you'll drink with it. Jamie recommends her Blanc de Blancs, which is a full-bodied sparkler made from Chardonnay, and I agree—that sort of wine is a better choice than a Blanc de Noir (from Pinot Noir), which is lighter.

⊰wine recommendation: blanc de blancs champagne⊱

Serves four

1 CUP CHAMPAGNE

½ CUP FISH BROTH OR CLAM JUICE

1 STALK CELERY WITH LEAVES ON, CHOPPED

1 SMALL ONION, CHOPPED

2 BAY LEAVES

4 TROUT, HEADLESS

¼ CUP HEAVY CREAM

1 TEASPOON FRESH LEMON JUICE

1 AVOCADO, PEELED, PITTED, AND MASHED TO A SMOOTH PASTE

1 BUNCH WATERCRESS, STEMMED

2 TABLESPOONS FINELY CHOPPED RED BELL PEPPER

2 TABLESPOONS MINCED FRESH CHIVES

~Preheat the oven to 350°F. In a small saucepan, combine the Champagne, fish broth or clam juice, celery, onion, and bay leaves and simmer for 15 minutes. Strain and discard the vegetables.

~Put the fish in a baking dish. Pour the poaching liquid over the trout, cover with aluminum foil, and bake for 15 minutes. Transfer the trout to a platter, cover with plastic wrap, and let cool.

~Strain the poaching liquid into a clean saucepan and simmer until reduced to about 1 cup. Off heat, whisk in the cream, lemon juice, and avocado until smooth. Let cool (if it separates, stir just before serving).

~Gently remove the skin from the trout and lift the fillets away from the spine. Place 2 fillets side by side on each warmed plate. Garnish with watercress, scatter the bell pepper and chives across the fish, and pour the sauce over.

TROUT FILLETS WITH SHALLOT SAUCE

In Alsace once, just before Christmas, my wife and I found ourselves stranded one lunchtime between appointments—there wasn't a single restaurant table available in Kaysersberg, whose Christmas market draws people from neighboring Germany and even Switzerland. A local wine maker recommended a small place in the mountains nearby, called Les Alisiers, and after a reassuring phone call, we took what turned out to be a long and very winding road up to a mountaintop, where a rainbow appeared as we were stepping into a nearly empty dining room. The lack of many other customers meant we could chat with our hostess, the chef's wife, and persuade her to give us this recipe. It was made with Alsatian Pinot Noir, which is extremely light, but makes a pretty and delicious sauce.

This is a regal sauce, similar to *beurre blanc*. Some recipes specify cream, which makes it a different thing, not as fine. Use the best ingredients: really good butter, first-rate vinegar, quite dry wine (a Zinfandel rosé or a good one from Provence, but not "white" Zinfandel or other sweet jug wine). Incidentally, this recipe proves that vinegar and wine needn't be kept apart; the vinegar simply needs to be good, and used judiciously. Steaming the fish keeps it juicy, with a smooth texture that suits the sauce. The wine needs to be bone-dry, acidic, and full. You can also use this sauce with salmon, in which case the best wine would be as acidic but fuller, such as first-class Chardonnay. Either way, it's a thoroughly elegant first course for a grand dinner.

◦{ wine recommendation: alsace riesling }◦

2 TABLESPOONS MINCED FRESH OREGANO

SALT AND FRESHLY GROUND PEPPER TO TASTE

4 TROUT, HEADLESS

4 BAY LEAVES

¼ CUP MINCED SHALLOTS

¼ CUP RED WINE VINEGAR

¼ CUP DRY ROSÉ WINE

1 CUP (2 sticks) COLD UNSALTED BUTTER, CUT INTO ½-INCH CUBES

2 TABLESPOONS MINCED FRESH CHIVES

SALAD GREENS, SUCH AS RADICCHIO LEAVES AND WATERCRESS SPRIGS, FOR GARNISH

Serves four

~Sprinkle the oregano, salt, and pepper inside each trout and insert 1 bay leaf in each. Set aside.

~To start the sauce: In a small saucepan (not nonstick), combine the shallots, vinegar, and wine and simmer, uncovered, until most of the liquid has evaporated, about 15 minutes. Remove from heat and set aside.

~In a covered steamer over rapidly simmering water (a Chinese bamboo steamer basket works well), steam the trout, side by side, for 6 minutes. Remove from heat. Carefully remove the skin and backbone from the fish. Transfer the fillets to a warm platter.

~Meanwhile, finish the sauce: Return the pan with the shallots to very low heat and begin whisking in the butter 1 chunk at a time. The sauce will become more and more creamy and silky as you whisk it. Pour some right from the pan onto 4 warmed plates, lay 2 fillets on each, and drizzle a bit more on top. Scatter the chives over, and garnish with salad leaves.

PRAWNS AND CHORIZO ON RISOTTO CAKES

A long time ago, I learned this idea from Portuguese friends, then eventually forgot it until I went to Spain, where I was delighted to be reminded: In Iberia, they sometimes make a cooking sauce by lightly frying sliced onion, garlic, and chopped chorizo, which releases some paprika-infused juices. In Portugal, it was mixed with clams; in Spain, it was vegetables. Either way, if you like a spicy bite, this is for you. It needs a starch, and the best idea is cross-cultural, pairing it with cakes made from leftover Green Herb Risotto (see page 88), although any vegetable risotto will do; we generally make a bit extra of the risotto, and have this for lunch with a salad or as part of a light supper the next day. The best wine is well-chilled dry rosé made principally from the Grenache grape.

⊰wine recommendation: bandol, navarra, australian rosé⊱

Serves four

2 CUPS COLD RISOTTO

4 TABLESPOONS OLIVE OIL

1 SMALL ONION, CHOPPED

4 OUNCES SPANISH CHORIZO, DICED

24 JUMBO SHRIMP, SHELLED AND DEVEINED

~Form the risotto into 4 patties, wrap each in plastic wrap, and chill in refrigerator overnight. Remove from the fridge 30 minutes before cooking.

~Heat 1 tablespoon of the olive oil in a skillet over medium heat and sauté the onion for about 5 minutes, or until soft and beginning to turn golden. Add the chorizo and cook, stirring, until it releases its juices. Turn heat off.

~Heat the remaining 3 tablespoons olive oil in a large nonstick skillet over medium-high heat. Carefully place the risotto cakes in the pan and cook until browned and slightly crisp, about 3 minutes on each side. Using a slotted metal spatula, transfer to paper towel to drain. Increase heat to high, and add the chorizo-onion mix and the shrimp. Sauté for about 2 minutes, or until shrimp are evenly pink. Remove from heat. Place 1 risotto cake on each of 4 warmed plates and top each with 6 shrimp and sauce.

PRAWNS BAKED WITH FETA CHEESE

Seafood cooked in tomato sauce, especially a really hearty preparation like cioppino and other fish stews, creates something of a fork in the gastronomic road: white or red? The answer really depends on your tolerance for acidity, as white wine will provide a good shot of pucker-power when like meets like. The easy, and quite tasty, solution is Zinfandel. Its robust flavor and abundant berry fruitiness actually tone down the acidity of tomato sauce, and are a good fit with the tang of feta cheese and basil. This recipe is from the Lolonis family in Mendocino, California, where they've been growing grapes and making wine for several generations.

{wine recommendation: zinfandel}

Serves six

2 TABLESPOONS EXTRA-VIRGIN OLIVE OIL

2 TEASPOONS MINCED GARLIC

¼ CUP DRY WHITE WINE

14 OUNCES CANNED PEELED PLUM TOMATOES IN JUICE, COARSELY CHOPPED

36 JUMBO SHRIMP (about 2 pounds), SHELLED AND DEVEINED

1 TEASPOON SALT

1 TEASPOON FRESHLY GROUND PEPPER

8 OUNCES FETA CHEESE, CRUMBLED (1½ cups)

3 TABLESPOONS CHOPPED FRESH BASIL

STEAMED RICE FOR SERVING

~Preheat the oven to 350°F. In a heavy, medium saucepan, heat the olive oil over medium heat and sauté the garlic for 1 or 2 minutes, or until fragrant. Add the wine and simmer for 2 minutes. Add the tomatoes and simmer for 15 minutes. Put the shrimp in a baking dish. Sprinkle the salt, pepper, feta cheese, and half the basil on top. Pour the tomato sauce over all. Cover with aluminum foil and bake for 15 minutes.

~Remove from the oven and sprinkle with remaining basil. Serve over steamed rice.

PETRALE DORÉ IN LEMON VELVET SAUCE

This was a favorite dish at the legendary Washington Square Bar & Grill in San Francisco, and it's sometimes now revived at Moose's, across the square from the old hangout. Mary Etta Moose says they now often make it with imported turbot, which is cheaper than the local but rare petrale; you could also use sand dabs (also known as American plaice), lemon sole, rex sole, or almost any good-quality flatfish. This recipe makes a little more sauce than you'll need, but it's the minimum quantity to easily work with—less wouldn't cook up as well. Serve with basmati rice, or a mix of half-and-half basmati rice and orzo pasta, tossed with a little butter. The wine needs to be light and very, very crisp.

◦{ wine recommendation: california sauvignon blanc, albariño }◦

Serves six

SAUCE:

2 TABLESPOONS UNSALTED BUTTER

3 TABLESPOONS ALL-PURPOSE FLOUR

1 CUP CANNED LOW-SALT CHICKEN BROTH, HEATED

¼ CUP FRESH LEMON JUICE

SALT AND FRESHLY GROUND PEPPER TO TASTE

1 LARGE EGG

½ CUP ALL-PURPOSE FLOUR

6 FLATFISH FILLETS, 6 TO 8 OUNCES EACH

SALT AND FRESHLY GROUND PEPPER TO TASTE

2 TABLESPOONS UNSALTED BUTTER

2 TABLESPOONS BRANDY

1 TABLESPOON CAPERS, DRAINED

~To make the sauce: In a small, heavy nonreactive saucepan, melt the butter over medium heat. Stir in the flour and whisk until it just begins to brown. Gradually whisk in the hot broth. Bring to a boil, then reduce heat and cook, whisking frequently, until thickened and smooth. Stir in the lemon juice, salt, and pepper. Remove from heat.

~Whisk the egg and flour together into a smooth batter. Season each fillet with salt and pepper and dip in the batter. In 2 large skillets, melt the butter over medium heat. (If you have only 1 large skillet, cook the fish in 2 batches.) Cook the fish, with the fillets not touching, for 2 minutes. Turn the fillets over and give the pan a good shake so they don't stick. Spoon 3 or 4 tablespoons of the sauce into the pan, shaking it to coat the fillets. Add the brandy and cook for 2 minutes. Serve 1 fillet on each of 6 warmed plates. Spoon on 1 tablespoon of sauce per fillet and garnish with capers.

SALMON FILLETS AND SPICY LENTIL SALAD

Using wine in a recipe makes it easy to add flavors to fish without overwhelming it, as the wine is a perfect matchmaker. In this recipe, the flavors are subtle, but definite; it's a good summer lunch or supper, or even a first course for a more elaborate dinner. In the pan and in your glass, use a fairly tart wine, crisp and fresh—cold fish dishes like this benefit from a spark of acidity.

◦{wine recommendation: sauvignon blanc }◦

Serves four

2 TABLESPOONS FENNEL SEEDS

1 TABLESPOON BLACK PEPPERCORNS

1 ONION, CUT INTO SLICES

FOUR 4-OUNCE SALMON FILLETS, PIN BONES REMOVED

2 CUPS DRY WHITE WINE

1 CUP FRENCH GREEN LENTILS (*lentilles du Puy*)

1 CUP DICED CARROT

1 CLOVE GARLIC, COARSELY CHOPPED

4 CUPS WATER

2 TABLESPOONS FRESH LEMON JUICE

4 TABLESPOONS EXTRA-VIRGIN OLIVE OIL

2 TABLESPOONS MINCED FRESH PARSLEY

1 TABLESPOON MINCED FRESH DILL

1 TEASPOON DIJON MUSTARD

PINCH OF SALT

1½ CUPS DICED CUCUMBER

LETTUCE LEAVES FOR SERVING

~Slightly crack the fennel seeds with a rolling pin to release their flavor. Put the fennel seeds, peppercorns, onion, salmon, and wine into a baking dish. Let sit at room temperature for 1 hour. Transfer the wine and flavorings to a wide pan. Bring to a low simmer and place the fish carefully into it (there should be enough wine to cover). Poach for 10 minutes; the flesh should be just firm. Using a slotted metal spatula, transfer the fish to a plate and let cool. Wrap tightly in plastic wrap and refrigerate for at least 1 hour or up to 2 hours.

~In a medium saucepan, combine the lentils, carrot, garlic, and water. Bring the water to an active simmer and cook for 30 minutes, or until the lentils are tender but still firm. Drain and rinse in cold water, then drain again. Mix the lemon juice, olive oil, parsley, dill, mustard, and salt together. Add to the lentils. Add cucumber and stir well. Cover and refrigerate for at least 1 hour, or overnight. To serve, make a shallow bed of the lentils on top of a few lettuce leaves, and top with the salmon.

WHOLE SALMON BRAISED IN RED WINE–PEPPERCORN SAUCE

There are a number of classic French fish stews using red wine, but this elegant special-occasion dish has been adapted from the technique for braising meat and is closer to a roast. The fish is cooked with the skin on, which helps to retain moisture. The best accompaniments are the simplest: boiled or mashed potatoes and some nice green vegetables like buttered spinach, or green beans, or sugar peas. The best wine is a medium-bodied, well-rounded, first-rate red.

⊰ wine recommendation: burgundy, carneros pinot noir, rioja reserva ⊱

Serves six

¼ CUP OLIVE OIL

1 WHOLE SALMON, 5 TO 6 POUNDS

1 LARGE CARROT, COARSELY CHOPPED

1 LARGE ONION, COARSELY CHOPPED

1 STALK CELERY, COARSELY CHOPPED

3 LARGE CLOVES GARLIC, COARSELY CHOPPED

1 CUP COARSELY CHOPPED TOMATOES

1½ CUPS DRY RED WINE

¼ CUP RED WINE VINEGAR

1 TABLESPOON BLACK PEPPERCORNS, CRACKED

1 BAY LEAF

4 SPRIGS THYME

2 TABLESPOONS UNSALTED BUTTER

1 TABLESPOON MINCED FRESH PARSLEY

SALT TO TASTE

~Preheat the oven to 350°F. Heat the olive oil in a roasting pan over high heat and sear the salmon on both sides (use 2 spatulas, or heavy tongs with the ends wrapped in a kitchen towel, to avoid breaking the skin when you turn the fish over). Remove the fish from the pan. Reduce heat to medium and add the carrot, onion, celery, and garlic. Cook for 2 or 3 minutes, then add the tomatoes and cook for about 5 minutes. Add the red wine and vinegar, stirring to scrape up any browned bits from the bottom of the pan. Add the peppercorns, bay leaf, and thyme. Return the fish to the pan. Cover with aluminum foil and place in the oven. Cook, basting 3 or 4 times with the pan liquid, for about 45 minutes; test for doneness by tugging at the dorsal fin on the salmon's back—it should come away easily.

~Transfer the fish to a plate and cover loosely with aluminum foil. Strain the pan liquid through a fine-mesh sieve into a saucepan, bring it to a boil, and cook for 2 minutes to reduce slightly. Lower heat to medium. Whisk in the butter, parsley, and salt.

~To serve the fish, make a crosswise cut with a large sharp knife alongside the tail and behind the head of the fish, then along the side of the backbone from head to tail. Work the knife into the cut, holding it parallel to the backbone, and slide the meat right off, sideways. Peel off the skin. Lift away the exposed backbone to reveal the other fillet. Remove from the pan, turn over, and peel off the skin. Cut both fillets crosswise into 6 serving pieces. Serve on warmed plates, with the sauce poured over.

ROASTED COD FILLETS ON FENNEL-ARUGULA PUREE

Pureed vegetables provide a simple but delicious accompaniment to meat and fish, especially when several flavors are combined. Here, the sweet and lightly spicy blend of fennel and arugula—a cross between a sauce and a green vegetable—is a boost for the fish (rice would finish off the plate perfectly). This recipe also works with fillets of any white fish, such as haddock, halibut, or even sea bass, if you can get them thick enough (more than 1 inch). The best wine pairing is fairly full-bodied, smooth, and not too acidic.

◦{wine recommendation: semillon, viognier, australian semchard}◦

Serves four

1½ CUPS CANNED LOW-SALT CHICKEN BROTH

1 LARGE BULB FENNEL, TRIMMED AND CHOPPED

2 CUPS LOOSELY PACKED ARUGULA

2 TABLESPOONS OLIVE OIL

1 TABLESPOON FRESH LEMON JUICE

1 CLOVE GARLIC, HALVED

4 COD FILLETS, ABOUT 8 OUNCES EACH

SALT AND FRESHLY GROUND PEPPER TO TASTE

STEAMED RICE FOR SERVING

~Preheat the oven to 425°F. In a medium saucepan, bring the broth to a vigorous simmer over medium heat and add the fennel. Reduce heat, cover, and simmer for 20 minutes. Add the arugula and simmer for 5 minutes. Using a spoon, transfer to a blender or food processor with a few tablespoons of the cooking liquid. Puree to a smooth, thick mush; if it seems too thick, add a little more liquid and process for another minute.

~While the vegetables are simmering, combine the oil, lemon juice, and garlic in a small saucepan and cook over low heat for about 5 minutes. Discard the garlic and pour some of the liquid into a roasting pan to coat the bottom. Put the fillets in the pan and pour the remaining liquid over them. Add salt and pepper. Roast for 10 to 12 minutes, or until the fish is firm to the touch. Spoon the puree onto 4 warmed plates, and place the fillets on top and the rice alongside.

GRILLED TUNA WITH LEMON-GINGER MARINADE

Firm and meaty, tuna was made for the grill, and for wine. Its distinctive, full flavor carries strong spices and condiments along quite nicely, too. To preserve the texture of the meat, tuna should always be cooked a little rare, so that it's moist and translucent in the middle. Serve with rice pilaf or mashed potatoes whipped with a little olive oil and shreds of fresh basil. The wine should be red, fruity, and fairly light, served cool; 30 minutes in the fridge will get it just right.

◦{wine recommendation: pinot noir, beaujolais, gigondas, vacqueyras}◦

Serves four

4 TUNA STEAKS, CUT 1 INCH THICK

½ CUP OLIVE OIL

¼ CUP FRESH LEMON JUICE

¼ CUP DRY SHERRY

2 TABLESPOONS DARK SOY SAUCE

2 TABLESPOONS MINCED PEELED FRESH GINGER

2 CLOVES GARLIC, MINCED

½ TEASPOON FRESHLY GROUND PEPPER

~Rinse the steaks and pat them dry. Place them in a small baking dish. Mix all the remaining ingredients together and pour over the fish. Turn several times to coat thoroughly. Cover and refrigerate for about 2 hours, turning once to keep the fish moist.

~Remove the fish from the refrigerator 30 minutes before cooking. Light a fire in a charcoal grill or preheat the broiler. Drain and transfer the fish to a platter; discard the remaining marinade. Place the fish on a well-oiled grill rack or on a broiler pan lined with aluminum foil. Grill or broil 4 to 6 inches from the heat source for about 3 minutes on each side, or until tuna is browned on the outside but still medium rare in the center.

HALIBUT AND MUSHROOM PACKETS

Mushrooms complement fish beautifully: They extend and enrich the flavor of fish without intruding on it. I was served this dish in Italy, and got a look at the fish before it was filleted; it was some sort of horrible-looking spiny bottom feeder, although it turned out to be delicious. Back home, I spotted some halibut steaks and decided to try them as an alternative, and they were even better. Serve these with basmati rice to soak up the sauce. The wine should be relatively high in acidity, not too oaky, and at least medium-bodied.

{ wine recommendation: mâcon-villages, semillon, medium-priced chardonnay }

6 HALIBUT STEAKS, ABOUT 1 INCH THICK

4 TABLESPOONS OLIVE OIL

10 OUNCES MUSHROOMS, THINLY SLICED

2 TABLESPOONS MINCED FRESH PARSLEY

2 TOMATOES, PEELED, SEEDED, AND
COARSELY CHOPPED

18 FRESH BASIL LEAVES, TORN, PLUS 6 WHOLE
LEAVES FOR GARNISH

½ CUP DRY WHITE WINE

Serves six

~Preheat the oven to 450°F. Cut 6 sheets of parchment paper into 12-inch rounds. Remove the fish from the refrigerator 30 minutes before cooking. Remove the skin around the edges.

~In a medium, heavy saucepan, heat 2 tablespoons of the olive oil over medium heat and sauté the mushrooms for 2 minutes. Add the parsley, tomatoes, and the torn leaves of basil. Stir well. Add the wine and simmer until most of the liquid has evaporated. Remove from heat.

~Brush the parchment rounds liberally with the remaining 2 tablespoons olive oil. Spoon the sauce equally onto each sheet, spreading it to the size of the fish. Place a fish steak on top of each, with a basil leaf pressed onto each one. Fold the edges of the paper over 2 or 3 times and crimp the folds to form an envelope. Place the packets in a baking dish and bake for 12 minutes.

~Serve by putting one packet on each plate, so guests can enjoy the aroma that bursts forth when the packets are opened (have an extra plate handy for the discarded paper).

GRILLED SKEWERED SWORDFISH WITH CUCUMBER

In Liguria, on the northwest coast of Italy, the sea breeze is livened up considerably by the aroma of basil wafting down from the hills: This is where the Ligurians invented pesto sauce, and their lavish use of it with several kinds of fish inspired this recipe (you can substitute halibut if swordfish isn't available). The local white wine is Vermentino, hard to find elsewhere, but a good substitute would be any choice that is light and fresh and crisp, but not too tart or assertive.

*{ wine recommendation: soave, pinot grigio, oregon
or alsatian pinot gris }*

SAUCE:

1 CUP LIGHTLY PACKED FRESH BASIL LEAVES

½ CUP OLIVE OIL

¼ CUP WHITE WINE VINEGAR

3 CLOVES GARLIC

2 TABLESPOONS MINCED FRESH CHIVES

½ TEASPOON FRESHLY GROUND PEPPER

1 POUND SWORDFISH, CUT INTO 1-BY-1½-INCH CHUNKS

2 OR 3 ZUCCHINI, CUT INTO ½-INCH CHUNKS

2 CUCUMBERS, PEELED, SEEDED, AND HALVED
LENGTHWISE, THEN CUT INTO ½-INCH CHUNKS

STEAMED RICE FOR SERVING

Serves four

~To make the sauce: In a blender or food processor, combine the basil, oil, vinegar, garlic, chives, and pepper. Puree until smooth. In a bowl, combine the fish chunks and the puree, tossing to coat well. Cover and refrigerate for at least 3 hours or up to 4 hours.

~Remove the fish from the refrigerator 30 minutes before cooking. Light a fire in a charcoal grill. Soak 4 long wooden skewers in water. Add the vegetables to the marinade and toss well. Let sit for 30 minutes.

~Drain the skewers. Thread the fish chunks onto the skewers alternately with the zucchini and cucumber. (This messy step is best done over a platter, with some paper towels handy. Discard any remaining marinade.)

~Place the skewers on a well-oiled grill rack and grill, turning several times, until the fish is opaque throughout, about 10 minutes (it's better if it's slightly underdone than overdone and dried out—test a chunk to see). Or, preheat the broiler and place the skewers on a broiler pan lined with aluminum foil. Broil 4 to 6 inches from the heat source, as above. Serve on a bed of steamed rice.

WHOLE FISH BAKED IN THYME-INFUSED SALT

This is an absurdly simple way to cook fish perfectly, as well as being an impressive party piece. It's taken for granted in many Mediterranean restaurants, where you get to pick your own fresh fish from a tub of ice without regard to species. This recipe works for any fish, though it's easier with a firm-fleshed type that will yield a couple of tender, moist fillets, such as red snapper, sea bass, striped bass, a thick rockfish, or even a small salmon. Despite appearances, the fish won't taste salty at all. In fact, the flavor is so subtle that I enhance it a bit; the wine in the salt adds a little aroma, while helping seal the crust. The lightness of the fish requires the same of the wine.

{wine recommendation: soave, pinot gris, albariño, gewürztraminer }

Serves four

1½ TO 2 POUNDS OF KOSHER SALT

½ CUP WHITE DRY VERMOUTH

3 SPRIGS THYME

1 WHOLE FISH, AT LEAST 2 POUNDS, CLEANED BUT NOT SCALED

1 LEMON, SLICED THIN

~Preheat the oven to 400°F. In a bowl, mix the salt and wine, just to moisten the salt. Choose an oval baking dish that will hold the fish, though it's all right if the tail hangs over the edge. Fill the bottom of the dish with ½ inch of the salt mixture. Scatter 2 sprigs of thyme on the salt and lay the fish on top. Fill the cavity of the fish with the other sprig of thyme and the lemon slices. Pour the remaining salt mixture over the fish until it's completely covered (don't worry if the tail sticks out). Bake for 30 minutes for a 2-pound fish, or 40 minutes for a 3-pounder.

~Remove from the oven. With the back of a large spoon, tap the crust lightly all over until it cracks, and take off the pieces of salt. If the skin comes away, fine; if not, lift and scrape it away with a sharp knife. Cut crosswise alongside the gills, then the center of the fish, then just ahead of the tail, then lengthwise along the backbone, and lift off each half of the top fillet and transfer to a warmed serving plate. Slide the knife under the exposed backbone and lift it off the bottom fillet, then cut the bottom fillet in half crosswise and lift carefully out to serve (the skin should stay behind, but if not, simply scrape the last bits off when it's on the serving plate).

Note: Any sort of salt will do, but you use a lot less, and thus save some money, if you use coarse kosher salt, which has large grains.

MEATS

The taste of red meat lowers the perceived level of tannin in a wine, which is why Cabernet Sauvignon, Zinfandel, Bordeaux blends, Barolo, and Barbaresco go so well with steak or lamb: The wine becomes more complementary. There's also the matter of texture; any of these wines can seem a bit chunky, just as a good piece of grilled steak does. Roast beef and filet mignon, however, have more of a tightly packed grain and are finely textured, which is why the classic choice is fine Burgundy or Pinot Noir, with a first-rate well-aged Rioja or a good Merlot close behind: They're all smooth and silky, and like goes with like.

Pork and veal are a lot more versatile, being pretty much white meat. Most of the time, the choice of wine will depend on the strength and intensity of the sauce, garnish (pork and prunes, for example, actually work best with a fruity, light red), and cooking method, as well as cultural logic: If you find schnitzel à la Holstein on a menu (breaded veal cutlet lightly fried and garnished with an egg and some anchovies), order German Riesling, whereas saltimbocca (veal cutlet overlaid with prosciutto and sometimes cheese) is better with Pinot Gris.

Game and venison, being strongly flavored and usually served with heavy-duty sauces, generally work best with straightforward, boldly flavored wines, which is where wines like Australian Cabernets, or Shiraz and blends thereof, come in. The closest thing to an all-purpose red tends to be a Merlot or a Chianti, both of which fit into several niches in all of the above. The good news is that there is enough savoriness and depth in meat-and-red matching to make for comfortable overlaps in quite a few ways.

CLASSIC BURGUNDY BEEF

The Burgundy region has a tradition of amplitude in cooking, a kind of old-fashioned grandmotherly largesse that suffuses its cuisine, and this rich beef stew is the best example of it: a comforting signature dish. The perfect match is also Burgundian, of course. A reasonable budget choice would be a good Merlot from Chile or California, which would be soft rather than ample, but would have the right sort of roundness to fit.

{wine recommendation: pinot noir}

Serves six

1 LARGE ONION, CHOPPED

2 CARROTS, CHOPPED

2 SPRIGS THYME

2 BAY LEAVES

3 CUPS DRY RED WINE

3 TABLESPOONS OLIVE OIL

2 POUNDS CHUCK, CUT INTO 1½-INCH CUBES

5 SLICES BACON, CHOPPED

16 SMALL ONIONS, PEELED

2 TABLESPOONS FLOUR

2 CLOVES GARLIC, CHOPPED

1 CUP BEEF BROTH

8 OUNCES BUTTON MUSHROOMS

SALT AND FRESHLY GROUND PEPPER TO TASTE

2 TABLESPOONS CHOPPED FRESH PARSLEY

BOILED POTATOES FOR SERVING

~In a glass bowl, combine the onion, carrots, herbs, wine, and 2 tablespoons of the olive oil. Add the beef, cover, and refrigerate for at least 6 hours or overnight. Remove the meat from the marinade and pat dry with paper towels. Strain the marinade, discard the vegetables, and reserve the liquid.

~In a large, heavy casserole or Dutch oven, heat the remaining 1 tablespoon olive oil over medium heat, add the bacon and whole onions, and cook for about 5 minutes, or until lightly browned, stirring occasionally. Using a slotted spoon, transfer to a dish. Increase the heat to medium-high and brown the meat in batches on all sides. Using a slotted spoon, transfer to a dish.

~Add the flour to the hot fat and stir vigorously. Return the beef to the pan and add the marinade, stirring well. Bring to a brisk simmer and add the garlic and broth. When the liquid bubbles, reduce heat to a low simmer, cover, and cook for 2 hours. Add the bacon, onion, mushrooms, salt, and pepper. Cook for another 30 minutes. Serve garnished with parsley and accompanied with boiled potatoes.

THE ULTIMATE POT ROAST (*BRASATO*)

Braised-beef dishes show up all across northern Italy, from simple to relatively fancy, but nobody exalts them as much as the Piedmontese, up in the northwestern corner of Italy: They're known for using Barolo, perhaps Italy's noblest wine, in the pot (or at least they were, before the rest of the world caught on and made it a very expensive special-occasion wine. These days, they're more likely to quietly use Barbera; that's what I do.). Back home, I found our lean beef a bit dry if it wasn't larded, but my friend Matt Kramer, who wrote a marvelous book called *A Passion for Piedmont,* gave me his solution: Use brisket, and slow-cook it for 8 hours. (You could cook it overnight, and reheat it later, but I usually make it on weekends, starting in the morning, to serve that evening.)

◦{wine recommendation: barolo, barbaresco}◦

Serves six

3 TABLESPOONS OLIVE OIL

2- TO 3-POUND BEEF BRISKET

2 BOTTLES BARBERA WINE

1 ONION, SLICED

1 LARGE CARROT, SLICED

¼ TEASPOON GROUND CINNAMON

2 LARGE SPRIGS ROSEMARY

BUTTERED EGG NOODLES FOR SERVING

~Preheat the oven to 300°F. Heat the olive oil in a heavy casserole or Dutch oven over medium-high heat and brown the meat on all sides. Remove from heat and add the wine, onion, carrot, cinnamon, and rosemary. Return to medium-high heat until it reaches a simmer. Cover with a sheet of aluminum foil, then a lid, and braise in the oven for 8 hours, or until very tender. Check occasionally to make sure the liquid level is up to top of the meat; add more wine if needed.

~Remove the pan from the oven and let the beef cool in its liquid for 15 or 20 minutes. Transfer the meat to a carving board. Strain the liquid into a saucepan and boil rapidly until thickened. Cut the meat into ½-inch-thick slices. Serve over egg noodles and spoon the sauce over.

PEPPERY BEEF CASSEROLE

Some spices argue with wine, while others get along just fine. Pepper can go either way: The wine just has to be firm, and they'll be compatible. In turn, pepper smooths out tannin a bit, making most wines seem a little fruitier. This is a dish for direct, assertive red wines with a little spiciness of their own, such as Châteauneuf-du-Pape, Hermitage, Côtes-du-Rhône, and others from the Rhône Valley in France, or California Syrah, Petite Sirah, and the Rhône-style blends made by Bonny Doon, Cline Cellars, and several other wineries, or Australian Shiraz, which is the same grape as Syrah but made a little rougher and funkier Down Under. Basically, this combination is robust comfort food with robust wine: nothing fancy, but generous, perfect matchmaking.

{wine recommendation: any of the above exuberant reds}

Serves six

1 TABLESPOON FENNEL SEEDS

1½ TABLESPOONS FRESHLY GROUND PEPPER

½ CUP OLIVE OIL

2 POUNDS CHUCK STEAK, CUBED

4 SLICES BACON, CHOPPED

1 ONION, CHOPPED

1 CUP CANNED LOW-SALT BEEF BROTH

2 CUPS DRY RED WINE

1 CUP TOMATOES, PEELED AND COARSELY CHOPPED

5 CLOVES GARLIC, COARSELY CHOPPED

2 BAY LEAVES

BUTTER AND BOILED POTATOES FOR SERVING

~In a large bowl, combine the fennel seeds, pepper, and oil. Add the beef and stir well. Cover and refrigerate overnight to tenderize and flavor the meat.

~Using a slotted spoon, transfer the beef to several layers of paper towels to drain; pat dry with more paper towels. Pour the oil that remains in the bowl into a large, heavy casserole or Dutch oven over medium-high heat and brown the meat for a few minutes, stirring vigorously; it's best to do it in a couple of batches, to be sure the meat browns uniformly. Transfer the beef to a bowl.

~Reduce heat to medium and sauté the chopped bacon for 3 to 4 minutes. Add the chopped onion and sauté 3 to 4 minutes longer, or until soft. Add the broth and red wine to the pan and stir to scrape up any browned bits from the bottom of the pan. Return the beef to the pan and add the tomatoes, garlic, and bay leaves. Bring to a boil, stirring well to combine the juices, then reduce heat and simmer for 1½ hours, or until tender. Discard the bay leaves. Serve over boiled potatoes that have been partially mashed with a dollop of butter, so there is plenty of hearty chunkiness to them.

MUSHROOM-RICH BEEF STEW

Zinfandel is a wonderful wine, but it tends to be fairly power-ful these days: The California sunshine results in fully ripe grapes. The rich, berry fruitiness doesn't quite mesh with dense, savory sauces, though, so I no longer use beef broth or demi-glace with stews and braises meant to go with it. Instead, I mix several techniques from different parts of French wine country to make a rich but fairly clear sauce, and the low heat and relatively short cooking time keeps the meat tender.

{ wine recommendation: zinfandel }

SPICED WINE:

1 TABLESPOON JUNIPER BERRIES

1 TABLESPOON BLACK PEPPERCORNS

1 TEASPOON WHOLE CLOVES

1 BOTTLE (750 ml) DRY RED WINE

2 CUPS BOILING WATER

1 OUNCE DRIED PORCINI MUSHROOMS

3 TABLESPOONS OLIVE OIL

1 ONION, CHOPPED

1 LARGE CARROT, CHOPPED

2 CLOVES GARLIC, CHOPPED

3 OUNCES PANCETTA, COARSELY CHOPPED

2 POUNDS CHUCK STEAK, CUBED

6 OUNCES FRESH MUSHROOMS, SLICED

1 TABLESPOON BALSAMIC VINEGAR

SALT AND FRESHLY GROUND PEPPER TO TASTE

1 TABLESPOON SUGAR

1 TEASPOON MINCED FRESH THYME

1 BAY LEAF

6 SHALLOTS (about 6 ounces), HALVED

EGG NOODLES FOR SERVING

2 TABLESPOONS MINCED FRESH PARSLEY

Serves six

~To make the spiced wine: Crack the juniper berries and pepper-corns by pressing on them with the side of a heavy knife. In a medium, heavy saucepan, combine the cracked spices, the cloves, and the wine. Bring the wine to a vigorous boil and cook for about 15 minutes, or until reduced to 2 cups. Strain and set aside.

~Meanwhile, pour the boiling water over the porcini mushrooms and let soak for 15 minutes. Remove the mushrooms and set aside; reserve 1 cup of the mushroom liquid.

~In a large, heavy pot or Dutch oven, heat 2 tablespoons of the olive oil over medium heat and brown the onion, carrot, garlic, and pancetta. Add the meat, turning and mixing thoroughly as it browns. Turn off heat. Stir in the fresh and dried mushrooms, spiced wine, reserved mushroom liquid, balsamic vinegar, salt, and pepper. Turn on heat again to medium, bring to a simmer, and reduce heat to very low, so that the stew barely simmers. Cook, covered, for 1 hour, or until the beef is very tender.

~Meanwhile, combine the sugar, thyme, bay leaf, and remaining 1 tablespoon olive oil in a small saucepan over medium-low heat. Add the shallots, and cook, stirring frequently, for about 20 minutes, or until golden brown. Stir into the stew so that they cook together the last 30 minutes. Discard the bay leaf. Serve over egg noodles and garnish with parsley.

BRAISED ROLLED BEEF WITH OLIVES

This is another of those Italian dishes that goes under several names, with hundreds of variations, and even uses different meats, all cuts that need long, slow cooking. It's suited to lean meat like flank steak, and the fillings are limited only by your imagination. I like it a bit pungent and biting, as a good companion to full-bodied reds with firm acidity.

{wine recommendation: cabernet sauvignon, zinfandel}

Serves six

1 FLANK STEAK, ABOUT 2 POUNDS

4 OUNCES PANCETTA, OR 4 THIN SLICES SMOKED BACON

6 CLOVES GARLIC, MINCED

1 TEASPOON FRESHLY GROUND PEPPER

2 CUPS PACKED FRESH SPINACH LEAVES, COARSELY CHOPPED

1 CUP PACKED FRESH ARUGULA, COARSELY CHOPPED

1 CUP GREEN OLIVES, FINELY CHOPPED

1 ONION, FINELY CHOPPED

1 LARGE CARROT

2 TABLESPOONS OLIVE OIL

1½ CUPS DRY RED WINE

½ CUP TOMATO PUREE

3 TABLESPOONS MINCED FRESH PARSLEY FOR GARNISH

BOILED POTATOES FOR SERVING

~Preheat oven to 375°F. Butterfly the steak by slicing it through the center sidewise with a sharp knife until it's almost cut through, and spread it open. Pound it flat lightly with a mallet, rolling pin, or bottom of a skillet. Lay the pancetta or bacon along the top with the grain of the meat. Sprinkle the garlic and pepper over the bacon, then spread with even layers of the spinach, arugula, olives, and onion, leaving a 1-inch border around all the sides. Place the carrot on top at one end and roll the meat up around it loosely, tucking the filling in toward the roll as you go. Secure the ends with toothpicks or skewers, and tie with 2 pieces of string.

~In a large Dutch oven or heavy flameproof casserole, heat the olive oil over high heat and brown the meat on all sides. Add the wine, cover, and braise in the oven until tender, 1½ to 2 hours, basting every 30 minutes.

~Remove the meat from the pan, place on a cutting board, seam-side down, cut the strings, and remove the toothpicks. Whisk the tomato puree into pan juices. Cut meat into 1-inch-thick cross-wise slices and put on warmed plates, cut-side up, so that the pattern of the roll shows. Spoon the pan juices over. Serve garnished with parsley and accompanied with boiled potatoes.

SLOW-BRAISED LAMB SHANKS

These are some of the cuts that restaurants grab first, so it's a good idea to make friends with your butcher (I give mine a first-rate bottle of wine from time to time, which has turned out to be a great investment). Lamb shanks look quite unpromising—dark and sheathed in muscle—but that protein melts into a tender, velvety succulence and a great depth of flavor with long, slow cooking—this is comfort food of a high order. It also deserves the best claret you've got, preferably one with five or six years of age; its astringency will nicely offset the richness of the meat and its smooth, thick juices.

◦{wine recommendation: bordeaux, cabernet sauvignon}◦

Serves six

3 TABLESPOONS OLIVE OIL

6 LAMB SHANKS

4 SHALLOTS, COARSELY CHOPPED

2 CARROTS, COARSELY CHOPPED

1 BULB FENNEL, TRIMMED AND COARSELY CHOPPED

1 STALK CELERY, COARSELY CHOPPED

6 CLOVES GARLIC, COARSELY CHOPPED

1 TABLESPOON MINCED FRESH THYME

1 TABLESPOON MINCED FRESH SAGE

1½ CUPS DRY RED WINE

2½ CUPS VEGETABLE BROTH (page 89)

2 TABLESPOONS TOMATO PUREE

RISOTTO OR MASHED POTATOES FOR SERVING

3 TABLESPOONS MINCED FRESH PARSLEY FOR GARNISH

~Preheat the oven to 325°F. In a large casserole or Dutch oven, heat the olive oil over medium heat and brown the lamb shanks 2 at a time, on all sides. Transfer the shanks to a plate. Add the shallots, carrots, fennel, celery, and garlic and sauté until the vegetables just begin to brown. Add the herbs and wine, stirring to scrape up any browned bits from the bottom of the pan. Return the shanks to the pan. Add the broth and tomato puree. (The liquid should just cover the meat.)

~Bring to a low simmer, cover, and braise until very tender, about 1½ hours. Check the level of the liquid after 1 hour, and add more broth if necessary.

~To serve, place a shank on a bed of risotto or mashed potatoes and pour a ladleful of sauce over, making sure it contains some of the cooked-down vegetables. Garnish with the parsley.

LEG OF LAMB ROASTED WITH PANCETTA AND HERBS

The best way to roast a leg of lamb medium-rare and tender is to cook it at high heat. This method uses a light wrap of pancetta, the mildly cured Italian bacon, which adds flavor of its own and acts as a seal for the herbs, while also keeping the meat from drying out. With this dish, assertive red wines really come into their own: The tannin and acidity volley with the richness of the meat and herbs, back and forth, back and forth, in an endless, delicious game.

{wine recommendation: cabernet sauvignon, chianti, rioja}

Serves four

2 TABLESPOONS MINCED FRESH PARSLEY

3 CLOVES GARLIC, MINCED

2 TABLESPOONS OLIVE OIL

GRATED ZEST AND JUICE OF 1 LEMON

1 TEASPOON SALT

10 THIN SLICES PANCETTA (about 4 ounces)

4 SPRIGS ROSEMARY

4 SPRIGS THYME

1 LEG OF LAMB (4 to 5 pounds), TRIMMED OF EXCESS FAT

¼ CUP DRY RED WINE

~Preheat the oven to 450°F. Mix the parsley, garlic, olive oil, lemon zest, lemon juice, and salt together. Rub all over the meat. On a cutting board, lay out slices of pancetta, slightly overlapping. Press the rosemary and thyme sprigs into the top and sides of the lamb and wrap the pancetta around the lamb. Tie in place with 2 lengths of string. Place on a rack in a roasting pan.

~Roast, uncovered, for 10 to 12 minutes per pound (it will be rather pink in the center at 10 minutes, medium pink at 12). Remove from the oven and turn off the oven. Transfer the lamb to a plate, cut the string, and remove and reserve the pancetta, which will be crisp. Discard the rosemary and thyme sprigs. Pour the cooking juices into a small saucepan. Put the lamb back in the pan, cover loosely with aluminum foil, and put in the turned-off oven to rest (this helps to make it tender).

~Place the pan of juices over medium-high heat and add the red wine. Cook at a brisk simmer for 5 minutes. Chop and crumble the pancetta into bits, add it to the sauce, and stir well. Cut the lamb into slices and serve on a warmed platter, with the sauce poured over.

PAN-ROASTED PORK TENDERLOIN WITH BASIL MINESTRONE

I had a version of this dish in the south of France, although it was called "minestrone" there. As that word is Italian for "hodge-podge," as well as "big soup," and in that area there's a lot of overlap of the cuisines, it did seem appropriate. It was made with rabbit, but I've substituted pork tenderloin because it's more widely available and has a little more flavor (and is certainly the tenderest type of pork in these lean-meat times). The vegetables should have the consistency of stew, and the pasta should be one of the small types, like tubettini, conchigliette, or the smallest macaroni, so as not to intrude too much—it's just there to add a little interest. The wine should be red and as rich and voluptuous as the stew.

{wine recommendation: cornas, gigondas, côtes-du-rhône villages, california syrah}

Serves four

1 PORK TENDERLOIN (about 1 pound)

2 CLOVES GARLIC, CRUSHED

2 TABLESPOONS MINCED FRESH THYME

3 TABLESPOONS OLIVE OIL

1 ONION, FINELY CHOPPED

1 CARROT, CHOPPED

1 STALK CELERY, FINELY CHOPPED

8 OUNCES SMALL SHAPED PASTA

1 CUP FRESH OR THAWED FROZEN PEAS

2 ZUCCHINI, COARSELY CHOPPED

1 RED BELL PEPPER, SEEDED, DERIBBED, AND CHOPPED

3 ROMA (plum) TOMATOES, PEELED, SEEDED, AND CHOPPED

2 TABLESPOONS PESTO SAUCE (page 69)

1½ CUPS CANNED LOW-SALT CHICKEN BROTH

~With a sharp knife, make 4 shallow crosswise cuts across the top of the tenderloin. Mix the garlic, thyme, and 2 tablespoons of the olive oil together. Rub this mixture into the pork. Roll plastic wrap around it and let sit for 1 hour.

~Preheat the oven to 350°F. Heat the remaining 1 tablespoon olive oil in a medium, heavy saucepan over low heat. Add the onion, carrot, and celery. Cover and cook for 15 minutes. Set aside.

~In a large pot of boiling salted water, cook the pasta for about 10 minutes, or until al dente. Drain, rinse with cold water, drain again, and set aside.

~Meanwhile, brown the tenderloin on all sides in an ovenproof skillet over medium heat. Place in the oven and bake for 15 minutes.

~Add the peas, zucchini, bell pepper, and tomatoes to the vegetables. Mix well and heat through. Stir the pesto sauce into the broth and add to the pan. Increase heat and simmer for 5 minutes. Add the pasta, stir well, and turn off heat. Cut the tenderloin into ¼-inch-thick crosswise slices. Serve in warmed bowls over a bed of the vegetable mixture.

APRICOT-STUFFED PORK WRAPPED IN PROSCIUTTO

Several countries with quite dissimilar cultures and cuisines have come up with the idea of combining pork and fruit: The Danes use prunes, the northern French use apples, and the southern Italians use raisins, for example. As much as I like them all, my preference is for something less sweet, and with a smoother sauce than many of those preparations. Sage seems to work best of all herbs with tart fruit, as this elegant preparation shows. Pork is often known as "the other white meat," and it lends itself well to white wine in a lot of simple preparations, like roasts, but here, because its taste is boosted by the flavor of the stuffing, my first choice would be a light, fruity red.

[wine recommendation: beaujolais, cabernet franc from washington or california, chinon, valpolicella superioré]

Serves four

⅓ CUP DRIED APRICOTS

1 TABLESPOON UNSALTED BUTTER

2 SHALLOTS, MINCED

1 TABLESPOON MINCED FRESH SAGE

3 TABLESPOONS PINE NUTS, COARSELY CHOPPED

½ CUP (4 ounces) MASCARPONE CHEESE

1 PORK TENDERLOIN, ABOUT 1 POUND

8 SLICES PROSCIUTTO

½ CUP DRY WHITE WINE

~Soak the apricots in warm water to cover for 2 hours. Drain and finely chop.

~Preheat the oven to 400°F. In a small saucepan over medium heat, melt the butter and sauté the shallots for 5 minutes, or until just golden. Remove from heat. In a small mixing bowl, combine the shallots, sage, pine nuts, apricots, and all but 1 tablespoon of the mascarpone. Mix well.

~Make a deep slit down the side of the tenderloin from end to end, cutting nearly all the way through. Open out and flatten a bit by pressing down hard on the butterflied meat. Spoon the stuffing along the middle of the cut. Lay the slices of prosciutto on the work surface, slightly overlapping, and place the tenderloin on top. Carefully wrap the tenderloin with the prosciutto. Tie the roll at intervals with 4 pieces of string.

~Put the meat in a small roasting pan and roast for 30 minutes, basting with the wine halfway through. Remove from the oven and let rest on a warmed platter.

~Over medium heat, bring the pan juices to a simmer and whisk in the remaining 1 tablespoon mascarpone. Whisk well. Remove from heat. Cut the strings and slice the tenderloin crosswise into 4 pieces. Place them flat on a platter and drizzle sauce over each piece.

SALTIMBOCCA

The Romans gave this combination of veal and ham its name because it is so delicious, they say, that it "jumps in your mouth." In Bologna, where the cooking is sumptuous, they make a more lavish version with cheese and sometimes a light egg-batter coating. In San Francisco's North Beach, where I learned how to make it, you could find both styles. Here's a lighter version of the dish; it's so light, even though fairly rich, that it works best with white wine, one that's fruity, not austere or too acidic, nor too light. Serve with small rice-shaped pasta (called *risone, riso,* or *orzo*), cooked in chicken broth, then drained and tossed with butter.

◦{wine recommendation: oregon pinot gris, pinot grigio from friuli or alto adige}◦

Serves eight

8 VEAL SCALLOPINE, ABOUT 6 OUNCES EACH

3 TABLESPOONS MINCED FRESH SAGE LEAVES

SALT AND FRESHLY GROUND PEPPER TO TASTE

8 SLICES PROSCIUTTO

2 TABLESPOONS UNSALTED BUTTER

2 TABLESPOONS FRESHLY GRATED PARMESAN CHEESE

¼ CUP MEDIUM-SWEET MARSALA WINE

~Put the veal between 2 pieces of waxed paper and pound it lightly with a meat mallet or the side of an empty wine bottle to make it thinner. Scatter sage leaves evenly on each slice. Sprinkle with salt and pepper. Lay a slice of prosciutto on top of each. Secure with a toothpick at each end.

~In a large sauté pan or skillet, melt the butter over medium-high heat. Sauté the meat in batches, prosciutto-side down, for 2 minutes, shaking the pan to keep it from sticking. Turn the meat over and scatter a little Parmesan over the top. Shake the pan well. Cook for 2 minutes. Transfer to warmed plates. Pour the Marsala into the pan and increase heat to high. Cook, stirring to scrape up the browned bits from the bottom of the pan, until reduced by half, 1 or 2 minutes. Pour a ribbon of the pan juices over each piece.

DESSERTS

Have you ever known any number of people, even just two or three, to completely agree on dessert? I haven't, either—there are just too many levels of affection for sweetness, too much cultural conditioning, and too many goodies handed out by grandparents when we were kids, not to mention the forcefulness with which chocoholics make their case. Add wine to the equation, and dessert often becomes the Bermuda Triangle of dinner—something to sail around. It's an unnecessary detour, however, as there are a multitude of perfect matches.

As noted in the dessert-wine section, a glorious variety of flavors, textures, and sweet intensities is available. What that means, basically, is that there's at least one wine for almost every dessert. Often, there are several. The exceptions are few, and even then probably based more on prejudice than anything else. I have only two real conflicts: ice cream, where I think its coldness and sweetness dominate, and uncooked fruit salads, because I think the different acid and sugar levels of mixed fruits can cause so much discord that they drown out the wine, even though they're refreshing on their own.

Another type of wine is made from concentrated grapes, but these are grapes that are allowed to dry when they're off the vine. The best example of this type is Vin Santo, made in Tuscany. White grapes are harvested and the bunches are hung from the rafters of barns for several months, until they're raisiny. They are then made into wine and aged in small barrels for a few years. Some of the wine evaporates while it's in the barrels, which concentrates it further and oxidizes it, giving it even more of an aged character, which can make it seem dry even though it retains a lot of sugar. The character of Vin Santo is wonderfully complex, but it's enjoyed in Italy in the simplest sort of way, served with hazelnut biscotti, the crisp twice-baked hard cookies you see all over northern Italy. They are dunked into a glass of wine to soften and soak up the flavor, then munched with great satisfaction.

Port is the other popular dessert wine, and for many people it's the ultimate after-dinner treat. It's a fortified wine, made sweet by adding brandy to the fermenting wine while it still has considerable sugar; the brandy stops the fermentation, creating a strongly flavored, very sweet, full-bodied, dense, powerful wine. Very expensive vintage-dated ports need aging, often for several decades, before they mellow out, but there are quite a few styles made for easier immediate consumption. Most port is red, rich, and dark, but tawny port—amber, lighter, and a bit less sweet—is also well work trying.

Red port is traditionally paired with Stilton or other blue cheeses: The powerfully sweet and powerfully salty-pungent flavors make a good, if slightly domineering, fit. A better match, perfect for holidays, is port and mince pie or fruitcake. Tawny port, on the other hand, is great with pumpkin pie. If you want to take the casual route, there's nothing like a piece of aged pecorino cheese, a pear, and a dozen walnuts in the shell for satisfying, ruminative pleasure.

Another theory about dessert wines and dessert is that the wine should stand alone as the only sweet thing on the table, or at the most, be accompanied with something simple, like cookies, or a few grapes and a pear and a little cheese. This is what I generally do at home with casual dinners, but it does seem like a letdown after an elegant dinner. I think the best solution is to let the occasion, and the stature of the wine, dictate the nature of the dessert. The basic guiding principle is that the dessert should never be sweeter than the wine: If it is, it will dominate and even diminish the wine's flavor.

CARAMELIZED UPSIDE-DOWN PEAR TART

This is really a version of the French tarte Tatin, of course, but livened up with a hint of aniseed, an idea I got from Provence, where they make a mushy pear tart to go with their wonderful, sweet Muscat-based wines. The spice adds a touch of its subtle but distinctive licorice perfume. The tart comes out looking lavish and lush, though not formally elegant, but tastes deep and rich.

This tart needs to be baked in a fairly heavy pan with sloping sides, so the crust can be tucked in. I have a copper pie pan that's perfect, and I've seen it done in a 10-inch skillet. The easiest way, though, may be to make it in a round gratin pan. When inverting it, be sure the plate is big and deep enough to surround the tart. This recipe may seem difficult but the result is spectacular.

◦{wine recommendation: sauternes}◦

Serves six

¾ CUP (1½ sticks) UNSALTED BUTTER

½ CUP SUPERFINE SUGAR

2 POUNDS BOSC OR ANJOU PEARS, PEELED, CORED, AND CUT INTO 8 SLICES EACH

¼ TEASPOON ANISEED

8 OUNCES THAWED FROZEN PUFF PASTRY

3 TABLESPOONS WATER

~Preheat the oven to 400°F. In a large, heavy skillet, melt half the butter over medium heat. Add ¼ cup of the sugar and cook until the syrup begins to brown, about 10 minutes. Add the pears and aniseed, and cook, shaking the pan and turning the pears to coat with syrup. Reduce heat to low, cover, and simmer for 20 minutes. Remove from heat. Using a slotted spoon, transfer the pears to a plate.

~On a lightly floured surface, roll the dough out to a 10-inch circle. Transfer to a small baking sheet and refrigerate.

~In a small saucepan, melt the remaining ¼ cup sugar in the water over medium-high heat. Simmer until it becomes a dark amber color, then add the remaining butter and whisk till smooth.

~Pour into a round gratin dish or a 10-inch ovenproof skillet. Place the pears in concentric circles on top of the syrup, leaving a little space around the edges for the dough. Place the circle of dough on top of the pears and tuck the edges down along the sides of the pan with the handle of a tablespoon. Press the top down lightly. Pierce the dough on top in several places, to let steam escape.

~Bake until browned, 20 to 25 minutes. Remove from oven and let cool for 10 minutes. Choose a large, rimmed plate big enough to hold the tart in its center. Place the plate on top of the tart, upside down. Hold with one hand on top of the plate and the other on the bottom of the tart pan or dish and quickly invert the tart onto the plate. Let cool for another 5 minutes, then remove the pan or dish. The tart will be a bit rustic and free-form, but that only makes it the genuine, handmade thing.

BAKED STUFFED PEACHES WITH RASPBERRY COULIS

For those who prefer their dessert wines a bit lighter than the super-sweet or fortified types, there are sparkling wines. Some sweet sparkling wine is made in France and Germany, but the main stream flows from Italy, in the form of Asti Spumante, which is made from the Muscat grape and carries its unmistakable spicy fragrance. It's relatively low in alcohol—about 9 percent—and only moderately effervescent, so it's a cool and easygoing end to a meal, especially nice on a warm evening. Serve it with a dessert like this and you'll capture the essence of summer.

◄{ wine recommendation: asti spumante }►

Serves six

3 PEACHES

8 AMARETTO COOKIES, FINELY CRUSHED

¼ CUP MEDIUM-SWEET MARSALA WINE

2 CUPS FRESH RASPBERRIES

½ CUP SUGAR

1 TABLESPOON WATER

~Preheat the oven to 400°F. Immerse the peaches in boiling water for 2 minutes. Drain and cool under cold running water. Gently slip off the skins. Cut the peaches in half and remove the pits. Enlarge the cavity of each half by scooping out about 1 tablespoon of flesh. Finely chop the flesh.

~Put the chopped peach flesh in a small mixing bowl with the cookie crumbs. Add the Marsala and mix well. Fill each cavity with a portion of the filling. If it seems dry, drizzle a little more Marsala over. Place the peaches in a lightly buttered baking dish and bake until tender, about 45 minutes. Remove from the oven.

~Meanwhile, make the coulis: Reserve 6 raspberries for garnishing. In a medium saucepan, combine the remaining berries, the sugar, and water and bring to a boil. Cook until the berries break down and a syrup forms. Strain through a fine-mesh sieve, pressing the berries through with the back of a large spoon. Discard the seeds. Taste for sweetness and add a little more sugar to taste if necessary.

~Place 1 peach half in each of 6 shallow bowls. Place 1 reserved raspberry on top of the filling on each, and spoon the coulis over. Let cool. Serve, within the hour, at room temperature.

VANILLA APPLE TART

Fruit tarts and pies are wonderful with late-harvest dessert wines, as they are light enough not to get in the way, but rich enough to be an interesting partner. There are no distractions about these desserts, either, no globs of cream, or overdecoration. One virtue of making your own tart, as opposed to running out to the local bakery, is that you know just how it will taste, and that it won't be too sweet or too tart to go with the wine. The apples I prefer to use are Pippins, Gravensteins, Granny Smiths, or Winesaps—any apple but Golden Delicious, which are too bland. This recipe came from Alsace, where they drink wonderful, spicy, late-harvest Gewürztraminer with it, but it's even better with late-harvest Riesling.

The pastry recipe is a basic sweetened dough, or as the French call it, *pâte brisée sucrée,* made here with a food processor, the home baker's best friend. It can also be made by hand.

◦⫯ wine recommendation: sweet riesling, sauternes ⫯◦

CRUST:

1½ CUPS UNBLEACHED ALL-PURPOSE FLOUR
½ CUP (1 stick) UNSALTED BUTTER,
WELL-CHILLED, CUT INTO 6 PIECES
1 TABLESPOON SUGAR
PINCH OF SALT
2 OR 3 TABLESPOONS ICE WATER

FILLING:

½ CUP (1 stick) UNSALTED BUTTER
½ CUP PACKED BROWN SUGAR
6 TART APPLES (see recipe introduction), PEELED, CORED, AND CUT INTO 8 SLICES EACH
1 CUP HALF-AND-HALF OR LIGHT CREAM
2 EGGS
1 TEASPOON VANILLA EXTRACT

Makes one 10-inch tart; serves six to eight

~To make the crust: In a food processor, combine all the ingredients except the water and pulse on and off until the mixture has the consistency of small peas, 10 or 15 seconds. With the machine running, gradually add water till the mixture forms a ball. Remove the dough. Place on a lightly floured surface and form into a ball, then flatten into a disk. Wrap in plastic and refrigerate for at least 1 hour, or up to 1 day. Preheat the oven to 400°F. On a lightly floured surface, roll the dough out into a 12-inch round. Fit into a 10-inch tart pan with a removable bottom. Run a rolling pin over the top edge to trim off the dough. Prick holes in the bottom with a fork. Line the tart with a piece of aluminum foil and fill with dried beans or pie weights. Bake until just set, about 15 minutes. Remove from the oven, remove the foil and weights, and let cool completely.

~To make the filling: Preheat the oven to 400°F. In a large, heavy skillet, melt the butter over medium heat. Add half the brown sugar and stir well. Add the apples and cook, shaking the pan occasionally, for about 10 minutes, or until softened and golden. Using a slotted spoon, transfer the apples to a bowl. Reduce heat and leave the syrup in the pan to caramelize slightly for about 2 minutes.

~Meanwhile, whisk the cream, remaining brown sugar, eggs, and vanilla extract together. Arrange the apples in the crust in concentric circles. Drizzle the caramelized syrup over them, then pour the cream mixture over. Bake until the top is set and lightly browned, about 30 minutes.

MARSALA AND GOAT-CHEESE CAKE

Marsala is a wonderful dessert wine, as is Malvasia: These two golden glories of Sicily are full bodied and mellow, tasting and smelling of spices and vanilla and toffee and sunshine. Look for versions labeled *superiore* or *riserva* to get the best quality. This cheesecake, which isn't quite as sweet as most and gets a nice lift from the tang of the goat cheese, will also match well with aged tawny port and the sweetest style of Madeira, known as Malmsey, which has some of the same flavor attributes.

{ wine recommendation: marsala, malvasia }

8 OUNCES AMARETTO COOKIES, CRUSHED INTO CRUMBS

2 TABLESPOONS HAZELNUTS, TOASTED, PEELED, AND FINELY CHOPPED (see page 66)

6 TABLESPOONS UNSALTED BUTTER, MELTED

3 LARGE EGGS

¼ CUP SUGAR

2 TABLESPOONS MEDIUM-SWEET MARSALA WINE

1 TEASPOON VANILLA EXTRACT

1 CUP (8 ounces) RICOTTA CHEESE AT ROOM TEMPERATURE

1 CUP (8 ounces) FRESH WHITE GOAT CHEESE AT ROOM TEMPERATURE

Serves six

~In a medium bowl, stir the cookie crumbs and nuts together. Add the butter and stir to combine well. Spread over the bottom of an 8-inch springform pan and press down with the back of a spoon. Refrigerate until firm, at least 1 hour.

~Have all the ingredients at room temperature. Preheat the oven to 375°F. In a small bowl, beat the eggs until frothy. Gradually beat in the sugar, then the wine and vanilla. In a medium bowl, combine the ricotta and goat cheese, whisking well. Stir in the egg mixture and blend well. Let rest a few minutes.

~Moisten a paper towel with vegetable oil and lightly wipe the sides of the baking pan, so the cheesecake will come away cleanly after it's baked. Pour the cheesecake mixture into the pan over the prepared base.

~Bake for 30 minutes. Reduce the oven temperature to 325°F and bake until a toothpick inserted 1 inch from the edge comes out clean, 25 to 30 minutes longer. The cake will still be slightly wobbly in the center, but will firm as it cools. Turn the oven off and leave the cake in it with the door open to slowly cool down for at least 1 hour, to prevent it from cracking. Transfer the pan to a wire rack and let cool completely, then refrigerate overnight. Every step deepens the flavor.

BREAD PUDDING FOR GROWN-UPS

Bread pudding is thought of as a British staple, but it was really the French who invented it; there is even a recipe from Lyons, just south of Burgundy, for *tarte à la mie de pain,* a sweet bread filling in a pie crust, which must be the ultimate incarnation! Bread pudding has now traveled around the world, in countless variations: I've had it in London filled with a thick layer of jam, in Asia made with coconut milk (not bad, either), and in San Francisco's North Beach, as made by Dante Benedetti at the old New Pisa, where it was more like a sourdough French toast extravaganza, better for breakfast than dessert.

This rich version is an elegant variation on the classic dish. The cream gives it body and smoothness, the apple provides a nice surprise and extra flavor, and a glaze at the end adds to its appearance. Some recipes call for brioche or other fancy breads, which I think is going too far for no good reason. A loaf of good, white bakery bread is fine. This is a perfectly delicious match with late-harvest Riesling; the fit is really extraordinary.

◦{ wine recommendation: sweet riesling }◦

Serves six

1 LOAF WHITE BREAD, 1 OR 2 DAYS OLD

3 TABLESPOONS UNSALTED BUTTER AT ROOM TEMPERATURE

3 CUPS MILK

2 CUPS HEAVY CREAM

PINCH OF SALT

2 VANILLA BEANS, HALVED LENGTHWISE

6 EGGS

1 CUP GRANULATED SUGAR

2 RED APPLES, NOT TOO TART, SUCH AS RED DELICIOUS, WINESAP, OR MACINTOSH

1/2 TEASPOON GROUND CINNAMON

1/4 CUP SUPERFINE SUGAR

~Preheat the oven to 375°F. Cut the bread into 1-inch-thick slices and trim the crusts. Trim the slices to fit neatly on the bottom of an 8-cup baking dish. Butter the bottom of the dish, and one side of the slices. Place in the dish, butter-side up.

~In a large saucepan, combine the milk, cream, salt, and vanilla beans. Bring to a boil. Turn off heat. Whisk the eggs and granulated sugar together. Add to the pan, whisk all the ingredients together, and set aside.

~Peel, core, and finely chop the apples. Scatter evenly across the bread slices. Sprinkle with the cinnamon. Pour the milk mixture over through a fine-mesh sieve. Discard the vanilla beans.

~Bake for 45 minutes, or until set. Just before serving, preheat the broiler. Sprinkle the surface of the pudding with the superfine sugar and run the pudding under the broiler for 1 or 2 minutes to create a brown glaze.

SAUCES AND OTHER MATCHMAKERS

A wide range of flavorings brings food and wine together, and sauces lead the parade, reliable and amiable matchmakers. The easiest way to help the harmony along is to use wine in the sauce, of course: For cream sauces, for example, try adding a little wine to the cream before stirring it into the pan. In some cases, the wine itself is pretty much the sauce, as when you deglaze a pan after cooking and add that liquid to the meat, which extends the flavor of both.

MARCHAND DU VIN SAUCE

Most wine-producing countries have several sauces based on the local wines; in many instances, several different sauces even have the same name. This one, from Bordeaux, is a good example: It's only one variation of a number of "wine-merchant's" sauces. It's especially good on grilled flank steak or other large, lean cuts of beef that are sliced before serving. It's best made fresh, while a charcoal fire gets going or a broiler is preheating. Cabernet Sauvignon or Bordeaux is the wine of choice to serve with it, unsurprisingly, and the sauce actually does mellow their tannins. The recipe here is ideal for 1 flank steak or London broil.

Makes about one cup

2 TABLESPOONS UNSALTED BUTTER

3 SHALLOTS, THINLY SLICED

1 SCANT TEASPOON FLOUR

1 CUP DRY RED WINE

½ CUP WARM WATER

FRESHLY GROUND PEPPER TO TASTE

~In a small, heavy saucepan, melt the butter over medium heat and sauté the shallots until translucent, 2 or 3 minutes. Whisk in the flour. Increase heat to medium-high, and whisk in the wine and water. Add the pepper and simmer until thickened and reduced, about 5 minutes. Remove from heat. Reheat, stirring for 1 minute, when the meat is ready. Slice the beef on a platter and spoon over the meat.

AROMATIC BROWN SAUCE

This recipe came from a good cook in Normandy, which is odd, as most sauces there are based on cider or various kinds of cream—it's apple and dairy country, and produces no wine. My wife and I go there for the peace and quiet, and the fish, which we buy right off the boats, but we were served this by a friend who roasted a guinea hen, which was tasty but dry, then softened it with a dollop of this sauce. Since then, we've used it with roasted pork, chicken, turkey thigh, even meat loaf. It's so quick and easy that it can be made while the meat is resting before being carved. The sweet tang of the tomato and the pronounced spicy aroma make it a good match with fairly bland meat and a sturdy white wine like Chardonnay, or a savory light red like Valpolicella Superiore.

Makes one cup

2 TABLESPOONS UNSALTED BUTTER

1 TABLESPOON FLOUR

2 TABLESPOONS TOMATO PUREE

1 CLOVE GARLIC, MINCED

¼ TEASPOON GROUND CINNAMON

¼ TEASPOON GROUND NUTMEG

½ TEASPOON DRIED THYME

½ CUP DRY WHITE WINE

½ CUP WARM WATER

~In a small, heavy saucepan, melt the butter over medium heat. Whisk in the flour, then the tomato puree and garlic. Stir in the spices and thyme, then gradually whisk in the wine and water. Simmer, whisking constantly, until thickened and smooth, 3 or 4 minutes. Serve separately, with meat.

RED PEPPER SAUCE

This is a simplified version of a Spanish sauce, good on grilled or broiled strong-flavored fish like tuna or swordfish or mackerel—it calms them down a bit, and its slight sweetness also acts as a counterpoint to tangy white wines.

Makes one and a half cups

1 TABLESPOON OLIVE OIL

2 RED BELL PEPPERS, SEEDED, DERIBBED, AND CUT INTO 2-INCH CHUNKS

2 SHALLOTS, COARSELY CHOPPED

1 CLOVE GARLIC, COARSELY CHOPPED

2 CUPS FISH BROTH OR CLAM JUICE

¼ CUP WHITE DRY VERMOUTH

2 TABLESPOONS SOFT RICOTTA CHEESE

~In a medium saucepan, heat the oil over medium-low heat and sauté the bell peppers, shallots, and garlic until tender but not browned, about 5 minutes. Add the broth or clam juice, increase heat to medium-high, and cook at a brisk simmer for 15 minutes. Add the vermouth.

~Remove from heat and puree in a blender or food processor. Return to medium-high heat and simmer until reduced by one-third. Whisk in the ricotta and serve warm.

BETTER THAN BUTTER

At any given time, there are always half a dozen small jars and plastic containers in my refrigerator and freezer, a collection of basics: salad dressing of various sorts, bases for sauces, leftover herbs I've mashed with olive oil and frozen, vegetables marinating in different flavorings—all the clutter of an improvisational cook. The only constant in there—the one thing I deliberately make ahead whenever I have time—is compound butter, one of the best friends a cook can have. Compound butters are merely butter mixed with flavorings and frozen, to be used in or as a sauce. The difference they can make in a dish is considerable. The simplest use is to put a thick slice on a piece of broiled meat or fish as it comes off the fire, so the butter melts on it, but an even better idea is to add it to wine, stock, or broth while deglazing a pan, which gives the butter a chance to melt and intensely flavor the pan juices.

One of the best uses for this butter: While sautéing fish, cut off a piece of frozen butter as big as your thumb. As soon as the fish is cooked, transfer it to a warmed plate. Increase heat under the pan to medium-high, add 2 table-spoons of dry white wine, and stir to scrape up any browned bits from the bottom of the pan. Add the butter and stir well while it melts and browns slightly, then pour it over fish. This is delicious with a rich wine like Chardonnay or white Burgundy.

HERB BUTTER

Makes about one half cup

2 TABLESPOONS MINCED FRESH PARSLEY
2 TABLESPOONS MINCED FRESH TARRAGON
½ CUP (1 stick) UNSALTED BUTTER
AT ROOM TEMPERATURE
2 TABLESPOONS FRESH LEMON JUICE
SALT AND PEPPER

~In a small bowl, work the herbs into the butter with the back of a spoon. Gradually mix in the lemon juice a little at a time, then blend in the salt and pepper. Turn the butter out on a sheet of plastic wrap and form into a log by rolling up the plastic and twisting the sides closed. Freeze for up to several weeks.

Variation: For stronger-flavored fish like swordfish or snapper, substitute minced fresh rosemary and chives for the above herbs, and serve with Sauvignon Blanc.

PIEDMONT BUTTER

Chef Tony Penado was born in Italy but eventually settled in San Francisco's North Beach and cooked in several good restaurants there. He was a generous teacher, happy to share his knowledge. He called this delicious butter after his native Piedmont, but I've never come across it there; most likely it came from the source of most good Italian cooking, an inspired *nonna* (grandma). Put a chunk of it on chicken or turkey or a veal chop just before serving, or stir it into the liquid after deglazing a sauté pan, for a quick sauce.

Makes about one half cup

½ CUP (1 stick) UNSALTED BUTTER
AT ROOM TEMPERATURE

2 HEAPING TABLESPOONS GRATED
PARMESAN CHEESE

GRATED ZEST OF 1 LEMON

3 OR 4 GRATINGS FRESH NUTMEG

~In a small bowl, cream the butter with the cheese, lemon zest, and nutmeg (fresh nutmeg is far more flavorful than packaged grated nutmeg). Roll the butter in plastic wrap and freeze for up to several weeks.

RED ONION MARMALADE

Here's another cook's friend, a versatile accompanist somewhere between a relish and a vegetable in itself. On most menus these days, slow-simmered vegetables like this are referred to as *confits,* shorthand for *confiture,* jam or preserves. It works very well as a relish, either at room temperature or warmed up, with ham, roast pork, or turkey and a light fruity red wine like Merlot, Beaujolais, or Dolcetto. (It's also good cold, served instead of cranberry sauce at Thanksgiving, or with leftover chicken.) The wine we use in it is usually whatever's left over, which is fine even after a few days. This can be made ahead and will keep for a couple of weeks in a jar in the fridge.

Makes about two cups

½ CUP (1 stick) UNSALTED BUTTER

1 POUND YELLOW ONIONS, PEELED AND THINLY SLICED

2 LARGE RED ONIONS, PEELED AND THINLY SLICED

1 TEASPOON SALT

1 TEASPOON FRESHLY GROUND PEPPER

2 TABLESPOONS HONEY

2 TABLESPOONS TOMATO PUREE

12 OIL-PACKED SUN-DRIED TOMATO HALVES,
DRAINED AND COARSELY CHOPPED

1 TEASPOON DRIED THYME

½ CUP BALSAMIC VINEGAR

1 CUP DRY RED WINE

~In a large, heavy saucepan, melt the butter over medium heat. Add all the remaining ingredients except the vinegar and wine. Stir well. Reduce heat to very low, cover, and cook, stirring occasionally, until the onions begin to brown, about 1 hour. Stir in the vinegar and wine. Cook, uncovered, until most of the liquid has evaporated and the mixture is a rich mahogany color, about 45 minutes longer. Let cool. Spoon into airtight jars, cover, and refrigerate for up to 2 weeks.

RECIPES AND
WINE RECOMMENDATIONS

*This is organized by wines, with
a list of recipes that match well.
The page numbers in bold-face refer
to their detailed flavor profiles.*

INDEX

Table of Equivalents

The exact equivalents in the following tables have been rounded for convenience.

Liquid/Dry Measures

U.S.	Metric
1/4 teaspoon	1.25 milliliters
1/2 teaspoon	2.5 milliliters
1 teaspoon	5 milliliters
1 tablespoon (3 teaspoons)	15 milliliters
1 fluid ounce (2 tablespoons)	30 milliliters
1/4 cup	60 milliliters
1/3 cup	80 milliliters
1/2 cup	120 milliliters
1 cup	240 milliliters
1 pint (2 cups)	480 milliliters
1 quart (4 cups, 32 ounces)	960 milliliters
1 gallon (4 quarts)	3.84 liters
1 ounce (by weight)	28 grams
1 pound	454 grams
2.2 pounds	1 kilogram

Length

U.S.	Metric
1/8 inch	3 millimeters
1/4 inch	6 millimeters
1/2 inch	12 millimeters
1 inch	2.5 centimeters

Oven Temperature

Fahrenheit	Celsius	Gas
250	120	1/2
275	140	1
300	150	2
325	160	3
350	180	4
375	190	5
400	200	6
425	220	7
450	230	8
475	240	9
500	260	10